St. Louis Marie de Montfort

TRUE DEVOTION

TO

THE BLESSED VIRGIN

or

Preparation

for the Reign of Jesus Christ

ISBN 0-910984-50-6 — Paper Edition

MONTFORT PUBLICATIONS
Bay Shore, N.Y. 11706

© MONTFORT PUBLICATIONS

1st Printing	1980	14,000
2nd Printing	1982	10,000
3rd Printing	1985	5,000
4th Printing	1985	5,000
5th Printing	1987	10,000
6th Printing	1991	10,000

Nihil obstat: R.J. Cuming, D.D., *Censor*
Imprimatur: David Norris, *rite delegato,*
Westminster, 21 November 1975
Imprimi potest: J.F. Matthews, S.M.M.
Superior Provincialis

Designed by John Harding

PUBLISHED IN THE U.S.A. WITH ECCLESIASTICAL PERMISSION

CONTENTS

BIOGRAPHICAL NOTE

Louis Marie Grignion was born in the village of Montfort in Brittany on 31st January 1673, but spent most of his childhood at Iffendic, a small town a few miles away. At the age of twelve he was sent to the Jesuit College of St. Thomas Becket at Rennes, where he remained for eight years.

The assurance that he was called to the priesthood came to him when he was praying before the statue of our Lady in the Carmelite church at Rennes, and unexpectedly an opportunity was offered to him to study in Paris. So at the age of twenty he set off for the capital, walking the whole 200 miles as an expression of the poverty he had joyfully embraced. He gave away all the money he had to beggars, as well as the new suit he had received. Then, kneeling down in the road, he resolved never to possess anything of his own but to rely entirely on the loving providence of his heavenly Father.

He began his studies at St. Sulpice and attended the university of Paris. Among many gifted and devout students, he was outstanding both for his intellectual abilities and for the holiness of his life.

After his ordination in 1700 his great desire was to go to the foreign missions, preferably to the new French colony of Canada, but his spiritual director advised against it, and he chose a life of missionary work in France.

All was not well with the French Church of his day. What especially troubled Fr. de Montfort was the lack of priests to minister to the people's needs, and the widespread ignorance of the faith. A short experience in the parishes caused him to write to his director, "Seeing the needs of the Church, I cannot help praying continually for a small society of poor priests who, under the protection of the Virgin Mary, will go from parish to parish, instructing the poor in the faith, relying solely on divine providence''.

That aim and desire remained with him throughout the years of his unceasing missionary work, as he walked from diocese to diocese. Because of his unconventional way of life, his outspoken condemnation of what was wrong, and his firm opposition to the erroneous doctrines of his day, he made many enemies. In fact, due to the intrigues of influential people, he was requested to leave more than one diocese and to carry on his ministry elsewhere.

On account of the disapproval he met in various places, he began to wonder whether he was following the path God wanted. For him there was only one way to find out. He would go to Rome and put the matter to the Holy Father himself.

As always, he travelled the thousand miles or so on foot, and on reaching Rome was able to have a private audience with the Pope. Clement XI, having heard his difficulties, assured him his vocation lay in evangelising France, and commissioned him to continue his missionary work — to catechise the children, to instruct the poor in the knowledge of their faith, and to encourage people to renew their baptismal promises, but always to work under the guidance of the diocesan authorities.

He left the Holy Father, his mind at rest, and endowed with the title of Missionary Apostolic to give authority to his teaching. There were only sixteen years between his ordination to the priesthood and his death, but they were full years. He went from parish to parish renewing the Catholic life of the West of France, preaching and instructing, providing for the poor, teaching catechism, organizing the building of shrines, renovating broken-down churches, and establishing schools.

All this strenuous apostolic work, added to his long journeys always on foot, his unceasing penances, and an attempt on his life by poisoning — all took their toll of his sturdy constitution. In 1716, while preaching a mission in the village of St-Laurent-sur-Sevre, he became gravely ill. He struggled into the pulpit to give his last sermon, which was significantly on the kindness of Jesus.

In the afternoon of April 28th it became evident that death was near. He kissed the crucifix and the little statue of our Lady which he held in his hands. Then he exclaimed, "In vain do you attack me; I am between Jesus and Mary. I have finished my course: all is over. I shall sin no more". Then he died peacefully.

Thousands came to pay him their respects before he was buried in St-Laurent, and ever since his tomb in the parish church has been a place of pilgrimage. He was canonized by Pope Pius XII on July 20th 1947, and his feast is kept on the anniversary of his death, April 28th.

The epitaph engraved in Latin on his tomb is an excellent summary of his life:

> You who pass this way, what do you see?
> A light quenched,
> A man consumed with the fire of charity,
> Who became all things to all men,
> Louis Marie Grignion de Montfort.
>
> If you would know his life, there was none more holy;
> If his penance, none more mortified;
> If his zeal, none more ardent;
> If his devotion to Mary, none more like Bernard.

A priest of Christ, he showed forth Christ in his
actions,
and preached him everywhere in his words;
unwearied, he rested only in the grave.

A father to the poor,
protector of orphans,
reconciler of sinners,
his glorious death was the image of his life.
As he lived, so did he die.

True Devotion to the Blessed Virgin

The spirit of St. Louis Marie still lives on; his
work and his teaching are continued by the priests and
brothers of his Company of Mary, as well as by the
Sisters of Wisdom and the teaching brothers of St.
Gabriel.

His writings, which were an extension of his
preaching, are the fruit of his deep study and constant
meditation. They can, perhaps, be summed up in three
words — Wisdom, the Cross, and Mary. Wisdom, for him,
is another name for Jesus, the Word of God, as proclaimed by St. John, the eternal Wisdom who became
man. In the thought of St. Louis, our aim in the
spiritual life is union with Christ-Wisdom; and in accordance with the plan of God, this necessarily involves the
Cross and Mary.

St. Louis Marie considered the role of our Lady
to be so important that he developed it in a book, which
is now known as *True Devotion to the Blessed Virgin*.
The manuscript of this was hidden during the French
Revolution and was lost for many years, until it was
providentially discovered in 1842. Unfortunately, the
first pages, including the title page, were missing. The
first editors gave it its present title, because one of the

author's aims was to distinguish true and genuine devotion from that which is false. However, over the years, the name "True Devotion" has been accepted as referring to that particular form of devotion which he develops and advocates in the second part of the book, and to which he gave the title "The Perfect Consecration to Jesus Christ".

So the book is divided into two main parts:
1) True devotion to our Lady in general — (Nos. 14-119).
2) The perfect true devotion, or holy slavery, — (Nos. 120-273).

In this edition we have added as sub-title that name given it by the Saint in No. 227, "Preparation for the Reign of Jesus Christ".

The work had a long preparation, since St. Louis Marie tells us that before writing it he had had discussions with the most saintly and learned people of his time, and had read almost every book that treated of devotion to Mary.

On reading his work, we cannot fail to be impressed by the author's familiarity with Holy Scripture and the writings of the Fathers. It is a mosaic of scriptural quotations, commentaries, references and reminiscences of numerous writers. Especially was he influenced by the exponents of the French school of spirituality, such as Berulle, Olier, St. John Eudes and Boudon.

He claims that his work is rooted in tradition and that this devotion "could not be condemned without undermining the foundations of Christianity." And he affirms that he has never known or heard of a practice of devotion to our Lady which is comparable to this one.

Its aim is to lead us to a closer union with Christ through a more faithful observance of our baptismal promises. It is not a question of saying some special or extra prayers to our Lady, but of living a life of total consecration to Jesus and his Mother, and for their glory.

His theological outlook and his style of writing may not suit everyone: he wrote some 250 years ago. A work written in an age and environment so different from our own will necessarily sound strange to modern ears. Certain expressions and comparisons may tend to put us off but, as Cardinal Suenens points out, St. Louis Marie's "theological formulations may surprise us, but we are indebted to him for a spiritual experience that has been the source of much grace" *(A New Pentecost, 1974)*.

And Father Faber, who first translated the book into English, says in his introduction, "I cannot think of a higher work or broader vocation for anyone than the simple spreading of this particular devotion of the Venerable Grignion de Montfort".

The reader who sets out to understand the basic and essential ideas in this book will be rewarded by finding an authentic spirituality, which will ensure growth in holiness and lead to a renewal of his Christian life, in harmony with the spiritual and Marian teaching given in our day by the II Vatican Council and the magisterium of the Church.

To quote the words of Pope John Paul II, addressed to the Montfort Family: "Be faithful to the spirit of your holy founder, to the inexhaustible fountainhead of spirituality which he left us, by teaching the meaning of true devotion to the Blessed Virgin." (Oct. 10, 1979)

ADDRESS OF POPE PIUS XII
on St. Louis Marie de Montfort

All the saints were undoubtedly great servants of Mary, and they all led souls to her. Grignion de Montfort is one of those saints who worked more ardently and more efficaciously to make her loved and served.

The greatest force behind all his apostolic ministry and his great secret for attracting and winning souls for Jesus was his devotion to Mary. All his activity depended on that devotion; in it he placed all his security; and he could not have found a more efficacious weapon for his age.

To the gloomy austerity, the sombre terror, the depressing pride of Jansenism he opposed the filial, trusting, ardent, expansive and effective love of the devout servant of Mary, of her who is the refuge of sinners, the Mother of divine grace, our life, our sweetness, and our hope. As our advocate, placed between God and the sinner, she takes it upon herself to invoke the clemency of the judge so as to temper his justice, to touch the heart of the sinner and to overcome his obstinacy. Convinced by his own personal experience of Mary's role, the missionary declared, with a picturesque simplicity all his own, that never did a sinner resist him after he had touched him with a rosary.

Moreover, it must be a sincere and loyal devotion. The author of *True Devotion to the Blessed Virgin* distinguishes in a few precise words this authentic devotion from the false and, to some extent, superstitious devotion, which consists only in exterior practices and superficial sentiment. Such a devotion leads those who cultivate it to live as they like and to remain in sin, presuming to receive an extraordinary grace at their last hour.

True devotion, traditional devotion, that of the Church, the devotion, we might say, of the good-intentioned Christian and Catholic, aims essentially at union with Jesus under the guidance of Mary. The form and practice of this devotion may vary according to time, place, and personal inclination. Within the bounds of sound and safe doctrine, of orthodoxy and dignity of worship, the Church leaves her children a just margin of liberty. She is conscious that true and perfect devotion to our Lady is not bound up in any particular modes in such a way that one of them can claim a monopoly over the others.

For this reason we ardently hope that in addition to the various manifestations of devotion to the Mother of God and of men, you will draw from the treasury of the writings and example of our saint that which constitutes the basis of his Marian devotion: his firm conviction of the powerful intercession of Mary, his resolute will to imitate as far as possible the virtues of the Virgin of virgins, and the great ardour of his love for her and for Jesus.

(Canonization of St. Louis Marie de Montfort)

Note. St. Louis Marie gives many of his quotations in the original Latin. For the convenience of the reader these have been transferred to 'Notes on the Text' at the end of the book.

St. Louis Marie de Montfort

TRUE DEVOTION

TO

THE BLESSED VIRGIN

or

Preparation
for the Reign of Jesus Christ

MONTFORT PUBLICATIONS
Bay Shore, N.Y. 11706

S.LVD. M
ONTFC

INTRODUCTION OF SAINT LOUIS MARIE

1. It was through the blessed Virgin Mary that Jesus Christ came into the world, and it is also through her that he must reign in the world.

2. Because Mary remained hidden during her life she is called by the Holy Spirit and the Church, *Alma Mater*, Mother hidden and unknown. So great was her humility that she desired nothing more upon earth than to remain unknown to herself and to others, and to be known only to God.

3. In answer to her prayers to remain hidden, poor and lowly, God was pleased to conceal her from nearly every other human creature in her conception, her birth, her life, her mysteries, her resurrection and assumption. Her own parents did not really know her; and the angels would often ask one another, "Who can she possibly be?",* for God had hidden her from them, or if he did reveal anything to them, it was nothing compared with what he withheld.

4. God the Father willed that she should perform no miracle during her life, at least no public one, although he had given her the power to do so. God the Son willed that she should speak very little although he had imparted his wisdom to her.

Even though Mary was his faithful spouse, God the Holy Spirit willed that his apostles and evangelists should say very little about her and then only as much as was necessary to make Jesus known.

5. Mary is the supreme masterpiece of Almighty God and he has reserved the knowledge and possession of her for himself. She is the glorious Mother of God the Son who chose to humble and conceal her during her lifetime in order to foster her humility. He called her

* Song of Songs 3:6; 8:5

"Woman" as if she were a stranger, although in his heart he esteemed and loved her above all men and angels. Mary is the sealed fountain* and the faithful spouse of the Holy Spirit where only he may enter. She is the sanctuary and resting-place of the Blessed Trinity where God dwells in greater and more divine splendour than anywhere else in the universe, not excluding his dwelling above the cherubim and seraphim. No creature, however pure, may enter there without being specially privileged.

6.   I declare with the saints: Mary is the earthly paradise of Jesus Christ the new Adam, where he became man by the power of the Holy Spirit, in order to accomplish in her wonders beyond our understanding. She is the vast and divine world of God where unutterable marvels and beauties are to be found. She is the magnificence of the Almighty where he hid his only Son, as in his own bosom, and with him everything that is most excellent and precious. What great and hidden things the all-powerful God has done for this wonderful creature, as she herself had to confess in spite of her great humility, "The Almighty has done great things for me". The world does not know these things because it is incapable and unworthy of knowing them.

7.   The saints have said wonderful things of Mary, the holy City of God, and, as they themselves admit, they were never more eloquent and more pleased than when they spoke of her. And yet they maintain that the height of her merits rising up to the throne of the Godhead cannot be measured; the greatness of the power which she wields over one who is God cannot be conceived; and the depths of her profound humility and all her virtues and graces cannot be sounded. What incomprehensible height! What indescribable breadth! What an impenetrable abyss!

*   Song of Songs 4:12.

8. Every day, from one end of the earth to the other, in the highest heaven and in the lowest abyss, all things preach, all things proclaim the wondrous Virgin Mary. The nine choirs of angels, men and women of every age, rank and religion, both good and evil, even the very devils themselves are compelled by the force of truth, willingly or unwillingly, to call her blessed.

According to St. Bonaventure, all the angels in heaven unceasingly call out to her: "Holy, holy, holy Mary, Virgin Mother of God". They greet her countless times each day with the angelic greeting, "Hail Mary", while prostrating themselves before her, begging her as a favour to honour them with one of her requests. According to St. Augustine, even St. Michael, though prince of all the heavenly court, is the most eager of all the angels to honour her and lead others to honour her. At all times he awaits the privilege of going at her word to the aid of one of her servants.

9. The whole world is filled with her glory, and this is especially true of Christian peoples, who have chosen her as guardian and protectress of kingdoms, provinces, dioceses, and towns. Many cathedrals are consecrated to God in her name. There is no church without an altar dedicated to her, no country or region without at least one of her miraculous images where all kinds of afflictions are cured and all sorts of benefits received. Many are the confraternities and associations honouring her as patron; many are the orders under her name and protection; many are the members of sodalities and religious of all congregations who voice her praises and make known her compassion. There is not a child who does not praise her by lisping a Hail Mary. There is scarcely a sinner, however hardened, who does not possess some spark of confidence in her. The very devils in hell, while fearing her, show her respect.

10. And yet in truth we must still say with the saints, *De Maria numquam satis:* We have still not praised, exalted, honoured, loved and served Mary adequately. She is worthy of even more praise, respect, love and service.

11. Moreover, we should repeat after the Holy Spirit, "All the glory of the king's daughter is within",* meaning that all the external glory which heaven and earth vie with each other to give her is nothing compared to what she has received interiorly from her Creator, namely a glory unknown to insignificant creatures like us, who cannot penetrate into the secrets of the king.

12. Finally, we must say in the words of the apostle Paul, "Eye has not seen, nor has ear heard, nor has the heart of man understood"† the beauty, the grandeur, the excellence of Mary, who is indeed a miracle of miracles of grace, nature and glory. "If you wish to understand the mother," says a saint, "then understand the Son. She is a worthy Mother of God". *Hic taceat omnis lingua:* Here let every tongue be silent.

13. My heart has dictated with special joy all that I have written to show that Mary has been unknown up till now, and that this is one of the reasons why Jesus Christ is not known as he should be. ¹ If then, as is certain, the knowledge and the kingdom of Jesus Christ must come into the world, it can only be as a necessary consequence of the knowledge and reign of Mary. She who first gave him to the world will establish his kingdom in the world.

---

* Ps.44:14.

† 1 Cor. 2:9.

¹ Montfort speaks here of practical knowledge, which is opposed to knowledge that is purely academic, dry and sterile.

PART I

TRUE DEVOTION TO OUR LADY IN GENERAL

CHAPTER ONE

NECESSITY OF DEVOTION TO OUR LADY

1. Mary's part in the Incarnation

14. With the whole Church I acknowledge that Mary, being a mere creature fashioned by the hands of God is, compared to his infinite majesty, less than an atom, or rather is simply nothing, since he alone can say, "I am he who is".* Consequently, this great Lord, who is ever independent and self-sufficient, never had and does not now have any absolute need of the Blessed Virgin for the accomplishment of his will and the manifestation of his glory. To do all things he has only to will them.

15. However, I declare that, considering things as they are, because God has decided to begin and accomplish his greatest works through the Blessed Virgin ever since he created her, we can safely believe that he will not change his plan in the time to come, for he is God and therefore does not change in his thoughts or his way of acting.†

16. God the Father gave his only Son to the world only through Mary. Whatever desires the patriarchs may have cherished, whatever entreaties the prophets and saints of the Old Law may have made for 4,000 years to obtain that treasure, it was Mary alone who merited it and found grace before God by the power of her prayers and the perfection of her virtues. "The world being unworthy," said St. Augustine, "to receive the Son of God directly from the hands of the Father, he gave his Son to Mary for the world to receive him from her".

---

* Exod. 3:14
† Heb. 1:12; Ps.101:28.

The Son of God became man for our salvation but only in Mary and through Mary.

God the Holy Spirit formed Jesus Christ in Mary but only after having asked her consent through one of the chief ministers of his court.

17. God the Father imparted to Mary his fruitfulness as far as a mere creature was capable of receiving it, to enable her to bring forth his Son and all the members of his mystical body.

18. God the Son came down into her virginal womb as a new Adam into his earthly paradise, to take his delight there and produce hidden wonders of grace.

God-made-man found freedom in imprisoning himself in her womb. He displayed power in allowing himself to be borne by this young maiden. He found his glory and that of his Father in hiding his splendours from all creatures here below and revealing them only to Mary. He glorified his independence and his majesty in depending upon this lovable virgin in his conception, his birth, his presentation in the temple, and in the thirty years of his hidden life. Even at his death she had to be present so that he might be united with her in one sacrifice and be immolated with her consent to the eternal Father, just as formerly Isaac was offered in sacrifice by Abraham when he accepted the will of God. It was Mary who nursed him, fed him, cared for him, reared him, and sacrificed him for us.

The Holy Spirit could not leave such wonderful and inconceivable dependence of God unmentioned in the Gospel, though he concealed almost all the wonderful things that Wisdom Incarnate did during his hidden life in order to bring home to us its infinite value and glory. Jesus gave more glory to God his Father by submitting to his Mother for thirty years than he would have given him had he converted the whole world by working the greatest miracles. How highly then do we glorify God when to please him we submit ourselves to Mary, taking Jesus as our sole model!

19. If we examine closely the remainder of the life of Jesus Christ, we see that he chose to begin his miracles through Mary. It was by her word that he sanctified St. John the Baptist in the womb of his mother, St. Elizabeth; no sooner had Mary spoken than John was sanctified. This was his first and greatest miracle of grace. At the wedding in Cana he changed water into wine at her humble prayer, and this was his first miracle in the order of nature. He began and continued his miracles through Mary and he will continue them through her until the end of time.

20. God the Holy Spirit, who does not produce any divine person, became fruitful through Mary whom he espoused. It was with her, in her and of her that he produced his masterpiece, God-made-man, and that he produces every day until the end of the world the members of the body of this adorable Head. For this reason the more he finds Mary, his dear and inseparable spouse, in a soul the more powerful and effective he becomes in producing Jesus Christ in that soul and that soul in Jesus Christ.

21. This does not mean that the Blessed Virgin confers on the Holy Spirit a fruitfulness which he does not already possess. Being God, he has the ability to produce just like the Father and the Son, although he does not use this power and so does not produce another divine person. But it does mean that the Holy Spirit chose to make use of our Blessed Lady, although he had no absolute need of her, in order to become actively fruitful in producing Jesus Christ and his members in her and by her. This is a mystery of grace unknown even to many of the most learned and spiritual of Christians.

2. Mary's part in the sanctification of souls

22. The plan adopted by the three persons of the Blessed Trinity in the Incarnation, the first coming of Jesus Christ, is adhered to each day in an invisible manner throughout the Church and they will pursue it to the end of time until the last coming of Jesus Christ.

23. God the Father gathered all the waters together and called them the seas or *maria*. He gathered all his grace together and called it Mary or *Maria*. The great God has a treasury or storehouse full of riches in which he has enclosed all that is beautiful, resplendent, rare, and precious, even his own Son. This immense treasury is none other than Mary whom the saints call the "treasury of the Lord". From her fulness all men are made rich.

24. God the Son imparted to his mother all that he gained by his life and death, namely, his infinite merits and his eminent virtues. He made her the treasurer of all his Father had given him as heritage. Through her he applies his merits to his members and through her he transmits his virtues and distributes his graces. She is his mystic channel, his aqueduct, through which he causes his mercies to flow gently and abundantly.

25. God the Holy Spirit entrusted his wondrous gifts to Mary, his faithful spouse, and chose her as the dispenser of all he possesses, so that she distributes all his gifts and graces to whom she wills, as much as she wills, how she wills and when she wills. No heavenly gift is given to men which does not pass through her virginal hands. Such indeed is the will of God, who has decreed that we should have all things through Mary, so that, making herself poor and lowly, and hiding herself in the depths of nothingness during her whole life, she might thus be enriched, exalted and honoured by almighty God.

Such are the views of the Church and the early Fathers.
26. Were I speaking to the so-called intellectuals of today, I would prove at great length by quoting Latin texts taken from Scripture and the Fathers of the Church all that I am now stating so simply. I could also instance solid proofs which can be read in full in Fr. Poire's book *The Triple Crown of the Blessed Virgin.* But I am speaking mainly for the poor and simple who have more good will and faith than the common run of scholars. As they believe more simply and more meritoriously, let me merely state the truth to them quite plainly without bothering to quote Latin passages which they would not understand. Nevertheless, I shall quote some texts as they occur to my mind as I go along.

27. Since grace enhances our human nature and glory adds a still greater perfection to grace, it is certain that our Lord remains in heaven just as much the Son of Mary as he was on earth. Consequently he has retained the submissiveness and obedience of the most perfect of all children towards the best of all mothers.

We must take care, however, not to consider this dependence as an abasement or imperfection in Jesus Christ. For Mary, infinitely inferior to her Son, who is God, does not command him in the same way as an earthly mother would command her child who is beneath her. Since she is completely transformed in God by that grace and glory which transforms all the saints in him, she does not ask or wish or do anything which is contrary to the eternal and unchangeable will of God. When therefore we read in the writings of St. Bernard, St. Bernardine, St. Bonaventure, and others that all in heaven and on earth, even God himself, is subject to the Blessed Virgin, they mean that the authority which God was pleased to give her is so great that she seems to have the same power as God. Her prayers and requests are so powerful with him that he accepts them as commands in the sense that he never resists his dear mother's prayer because it is always humble and conformed to his will.

Moses by the power of his prayer curbed God's anger against the Israelites so effectively that the infinitely great and merciful Lord was unable to withstand him and asked Moses to let him be angry and punish that rebellious people. How much greater, then, will be the prayer of the humble Virgin Mary, worthy Mother of God, which is more powerful with the King of heaven than the prayers and intercession of all the angels and saints in heaven and on earth!

28.   Mary has authority over the angels and the blessed in heaven. As a reward for her great humility, God gave her the power and the mission of assigning to saints the thrones made vacant by the apostate angels who fell away through pride.

Such is the will of almighty God who exalts the humble, that the powers of heaven, earth and hell, willingly or unwillingly, must obey the commands of the humble Virgin Mary. For God has made her queen of heaven and earth, leader of his armies, keeper of his treasures, dispenser of his graces, worker of his wonders, restorer of the human race, mediatrix on behalf of men, destroyer of his enemies, and faithful associate in his great works and triumphs.

29.   God the Father wishes Mary to be the mother of his children until the end of time and so he says to her, "Dwell in Jacob",* that is to say, take up your abode permanently in my children, in my holy ones represented by Jacob, and not in the children of the devil and sinners represented by Esau.

30.   Just as in natural and bodily generation there is a father and a mother, so in the supernatural and spiritual generation there is a father who is God and a mother

* Ecclus. 24:13.

who is Mary. All true children of God have God for their father and Mary for their mother; anyone who does not have Mary for his mother, does not have God for his father. This is why the reprobate, such as heretics and schismatics, who hate, despise or ignore the Blessed Virgin, do not have God for their father though they arrogantly claim they have, because they do not have Mary for their mother. Indeed if they had her for their mother they would love and honour her as good and true children naturally love and honour the mother who gave them life.

An infallible and unmistakeable sign by which we can distinguish a heretic, a man of false doctrine, an enemy of God, from one of God's true friends is that the heretic and the hardened sinner show nothing but contempt and indifference for our Lady, and endeavour, by word and example, openly or insidiously — sometimes under specious pretexts — to belittle the love and veneration shown to her. God the Father has not told Mary to dwell in them because they are, alas, other Esaus.

31. God the Son wishes to form himself, and, in a manner of speaking, become incarnate every day in his members through his dear Mother. To her he said, "Take Israel for your inheritance".* It is as if he said, God the Father has given me as heritage all the nations of the earth, all men good and evil, predestinate and reprobate. To the good I shall be father and advocate, to the bad a just avenger, but to all I shall be a judge. But you, my dear mother, will have for your heritage and possession only the predestinate represented by Israel. As their loving mother, you will give them birth, feed them and rear them. As their queen, you will lead, govern and defend them.

* Ecclus. 24:13.

32. "This one and that one were born in her".* According to the explanation of some of the Fathers, the first man born of Mary is the God-man, Jesus Christ. The second is simply man, child of God and Mary by adoption. If Jesus Christ, the head of mankind, is born of her, the predestinate, who are members of this head, must also as a necessary consequence be born of her. One and the same mother does not give birth to the head without the members nor to the members without the head, for these would be monsters in the order of nature. In the order of grace likewise the head and the members are born of the same mother. If a member of the mystical body of Christ, that is, one of the predestinate, were born of a mother other than Mary who gave birth to the head, he would not be one of the predestinate, nor a member of Jesus Christ, but a monster in the order of grace.

33. Moreover, Jesus is still as much as ever the fruit of Mary, as heaven and earth repeat thousands of times a day, "Blessed is the fruit of thy womb, Jesus." It is therefore certain that Jesus is the fruit and gift of Mary for every single man who possesses him, just as truly as he is for all mankind. Consequently, if any of the faithful have Jesus formed in their heart they can boldly say, "It is thanks to Mary that what I possess is Jesus, her fruit, and without her I would not have him." We can attribute more truly to her what St. Paul said of himself, "I am in labour again with all the children of God until Jesus Christ, my Son, is formed in them to the fulness of his age."† St. Augustine, surpassing himself as well as all that I have said so far, affirms that in order to be conformed to the image of the Son of God all the predestinate, while in this world, are hidden in the womb of the Blessed Virgin where they are pro-

* Ps.86:5.   † Gal.4:19; Eph.4:13.

tected, nourished, cared for and developed by this good Mother, until the day she brings them forth to a life of glory after death, which the Church calls the birthday of the just. This is indeed a mystery of grace unknown to the reprobate and little known even to the predestinate.

34. God the Holy Spirit wishes to fashion his chosen ones in and through Mary. He tells her, "My well-beloved, my spouse, let all your virtues take root in my chosen ones* that they may grow from strength to strength and from grace to grace. When you were living on earth, practising the most sublime virtues, I was so pleased with you that I still desire to find you on earth without your ceasing to be in heaven. Reproduce yourself then in my chosen ones, so that I may have the joy of seeing in them the roots of your invincible faith, profound humility, total mortification, sublime prayer, ardent charity, your firm hope and all your virtues. You are always my spouse, as faithful, pure, and fruitful as ever. May your faith give me believers; your purity, virgins; your fruitfulness, elect and living temples."

35. When Mary has taken root in a soul she produces in it wonders of grace which only she can produce; for she alone is the fruitful virgin who never had and never will have her equal in purity and fruitfulness. Together with the Holy Spirit Mary produced the greatest thing that ever was or ever will be: a God-man. She will consequently produce the marvels which will be seen in the latter times. The formation and the education of the great saints who will come at the end of the world are reserved to her, for only this singular and wondrous virgin can produce in union with the Holy Spirit singular and wondrous things.

36. When the Holy Spirit, her spouse, finds Mary in a soul, he hastens there and enters fully into it. He gives

* Ecclus. 24:13.

himself generously to that soul according to the place it has given to his spouse. One of the main reasons why the Holy Spirit does not now work striking wonders in souls is that he fails to find in them a sufficiently close union with his faithful and inseparable spouse. I say "inseparable spouse", for from the moment the substantial love of the Father and the Son espoused Mary to form Jesus, the head of the elect, and Jesus in the elect, he has never disowned her, for she has always been faithful and fruitful.

3. Consequences

37. We must obviously conclude from what I have just said:

First, that Mary has received from God a far-reaching dominion over the souls of the elect. Otherwise she could not make her dwelling-place in them as God the Father has ordered her to do, and she could not conceive them, nourish them, and bring them forth to eternal life as their mother. She could not have them for her inheritance and her possession and form them in Jesus and Jesus in them. She could not implant in their heart the roots of her virtues, nor be the inseparable associate of the Holy Spirit in all these works of grace. None of these things, I repeat, could she do unless she had received from the Almighty rights and authority over their souls. For God, having given her power over his only-begotten and natural Son, also gave her power over his adopted children, not only in what concerns their body — which would be of little account — but also in what concerns their soul.

38. Mary is the Queen of heaven and earth by grace as Jesus is king by nature and by conquest. But as the kingdom of Jesus Christ exists primarily in the heart or interior of man, according to the words of the Gospel, "The kingdom of God is within you", so the kingdom of the Blessed Virgin is principally in the interior of man, that is, in his soul. It is principally in souls that she is glorified with her Son more than in any visible creatures. So we may call her, as the saints do, *Queen of our hearts.*

39. Secondly, we must conclude that, being necessary to God by a necessity which is called 'hypothetical', (that is, because God so willed it), the Blessed Virgin is all the more necessary for men to attain their final end. Consequently we must not place devotion to her on the same level as devotion to the other saints as if it were merely something optional.

40. The pious and learned Jesuit, Suarez, Justus Lipsuis, a devout and erudite theologian of Louvain, and many others have proved incontestably that devotion to our Blessed Lady is necessary to attain salvation. This they show from the teaching of the Fathers, notably St. Augustine, St. Ephrem, deacon of Edessa, St. Cyril of Jerusalem, St. Germanus of Constantinople, St. John Damascene, St. Anselm, St. Bernard, St. Bernardine, St. Thomas and St. Bonaventure. Even according to Aescalampadius and other heretics, lack of esteem and love for the Virgin Mary is an infallible sign of God's disapproval. On the other hand, to be entirely and genuinely devoted to her is a sure sign of God's approval.

41. The types and texts of the Old and New Testaments prove the truth of this, the opinions and examples of the saints confirm it, and reason and experience teach and demonstrate it. Even the devil and his followers, forced by the evidence of the truth, were frequently obliged against their will to admit it. For brevity's sake, I shall quote one only of the many passages which I have collected from the Fathers and Doctors of the Church to support this truth. "Devotion to you, O

Blessed Virgin, is a means of salvation which God gives to those whom he wishes to save'' (St. John Damascene).

42. I could tell many stories in evidence of what I have just said.

1) One is recorded in the chronicles of St. Francis. The saint saw in ecstasy an immense ladder reaching to heaven, at the top of which stood the Blessed Virgin. This is the ladder, he was told, by which we must all go to heaven.

2) There is another related in the Chronicles of St. Dominic. Near Carcassonne, where St. Dominic was preaching the Rosary, there was an unfortunate heretic who was possessed by a multitude of devils. These evil spirits to their confusion were compelled at the command of our Lady to confess many great and consoling truths concerning devotion to her. They did so clearly and forcibly that, however weak our devotion to our Lady may be, we cannot read this authentic story containing such an unwilling tribute paid by the devils to devotion to our Lady without shedding tears of joy.

43. If devotion to the Blessed Virgin is necessary for all men simply to work out their salvation, it is even more necessary for those who are called to a special perfection. I do not believe that anyone can acquire intimate union with our Lord and perfect fidelity to the Holy Spirit without a very close union with the most Blessed Virgin and an absolute dependence on her support.

44. Mary alone found grace before God without the help of any other creature. All those who have since found grace before God have found it only through her.

She was full of grace when she was greeted by the Archangel Gabriel and was filled with grace to overflowing by the Holy Spirit when he so mysteriously overshadowed her. From day to day, from moment to moment, she increased so much this twofold plenitude that she attained an immense and inconceivable degree of grace. So much so, that the Almighty made her the sole custodian of his treasures and the sole dispenser of his graces. She can lead them along the narrow path to heaven and guide them through the narrow gate to life. She can give a royal throne, sceptre and crown to whom she wishes. Jesus is always and everywhere the fruit and Son of Mary and Mary is everywhere the genuine tree that bears that Fruit of life, the true Mother who bears that Son.

45. To Mary alone God gave the keys of the cellars of divine love and the ability to enter the most sublime and secret ways of perfection, and lead others along them. Mary alone gives to the unfortunate children of unfaithful Eve entry into that earthly paradise where they may walk pleasantly with God and be safely hidden from their enemies. There they can feed without fear of death on the delicious fruit of the tree of life and the tree of knowledge of good and evil. They can drink copiously the heavenly waters of that beauteous fountain which gushes forth in such abundance. As she is herself the earthly paradise, that virgin and blessed land from which sinful Adam and Eve were expelled, she lets only those whom she chooses enter her domain in order to make them saints.

46. All the rich among the people,* to use an expression of the Holy Spirit as explained by St. Bernard, all the rich among the people will look pleadingly upon your countenance throughout all ages and particularly

* Ps.44:13.

as the world draws to its end. This means that the greatest saints, those richest in grace and virtue, will be the most assiduous in praying to the most Blessed Virgin, looking up to her as the perfect model to imitate and as a powerful helper to assist them.

47. I said that this will happen especially towards the end of the world, and indeed soon, because Almighty God and his holy Mother are to raise up great saints who will surpass in holiness most other saints as much as the cedars of Lebanon tower above little shrubs. This has been revealed to a holy soul whose life has been written by M. de Renty.

48. These great souls filled with grace and zeal will be chosen to oppose the enemies of God who are raging on all sides. They will be exceptionally devoted to the Blessed Virgin. Illumined by her light, strengthened by her food, guided by her spirit, supported by her arm, sheltered under her protection, they will fight with one hand and build with the other.* With one hand they will give battle, overthrowing and crushing heretics and their heresies, schismatics and their schisms, idolaters and their idolatries, sinners and their wickedness. With the other hand they will build the temple of the true Solomon and the mystical city of God, namely, the Blessed Virgin, who is called by the Fathers of the Church the *Temple of Solomon* and the *City of God.*† By word and example they will draw all men to a true devotion to her and though this will make them many enemies, it will also bring about many victories and much glory to God alone. This is what God revealed to St. Vincent Ferrer, that outstanding apostle of his day, as he has amply shown in one of his works.

This seems to have been foretold by the Holy Spirit in Psalm 58: "The Lord will reign in Jacob and

---

* Nehem. 4:17.   † Ps.86:3.

all the ends of the earth. They will be converted towards evening and they will be as hungry as dogs and they will go around the city to find something to eat." This city around which men will roam at the end of the world seeking conversion and the appeasement of the hunger they have for justice is the Blessed Virgin, who is called by the Holy Spirit the *City of God.*

4. Mary's part in the latter times

49. The salvation of the world began through Mary and through her it must be accomplished. Mary scarcely appeared in the first coming of Jesus Christ so that men, as yet insufficiently instructed and enlightened concerning the person of her Son, might not wander from the truth by becoming too strongly attached to her. This would apparently have happened if she had been known, on account of the wondrous charms with which the Almighty had endowed even her outward appearance. So true is this that St. Denis the Areopagite tells us in his writings that when he saw her he would have taken her for a goddess, because of her incomparable beauty, had not his well-grounded faith taught him otherwise. But in the second coming of Jesus Christ, Mary must be known and openly revealed by the Holy Spirit so that Jesus may be known, loved and served through her. The reasons which moved the Holy Spirit to hide his spouse during her life and to reveal but very little of her since the first preaching of the gospel exist no longer.

1) God wishes to make Mary better known in the latter times.

50. God wishes therefore to reveal Mary, his masterpiece, and make her more known in these latter times:

a) Because she kept herself hidden in this world and in her great humility considered herself lower than dust, having obtained from God, his apostles and evangelists the favour of not being made known.

b) Because, as Mary is not only God's master-piece of glory in heaven, but also his masterpiece of grace on earth, he wishes to be glorified and praised because of her by those living upon earth.

c) Since she is the dawn which precedes and discloses the Sun of Justice, Jesus Christ, she must be known and acknowledged so that Jesus may be known and acknowledged.

d) As she was the way by which Jesus first came to us, she will again be the way by which he will come to us the second time though not in the same manner.

e) Since she is the sure means, the direct and immaculate way to Jesus and the perfect guide to him, it is through her that souls who are to shine forth in sanctity, must find him. He who finds Mary finds life,* that is, Jesus Christ who is the way, the truth and the life. But no one can find Mary who does not look for her. No one can look for her who does not know her, for no one seeks or desires something unknown. Mary then must be better known than ever for the deeper understanding and the greater glory of the Blessed Trinity.

f) In these latter times Mary must shine forth more than ever in mercy, power and grace: *in mercy,* to bring back and welcome lovingly the poor sinners and wanderers who are to be converted and return to the Catholic Church; *in power,* to combat the enemies of God who will rise up menacingly to seduce and crush by promises and threats all those who oppose them; finally, she must shine forth *in grace* to inspire and support the valiant soldiers and loyal servants of Jesus

* Prov.8:35.

Christ who are fighting for his cause.

g) Lastly, Mary must become as terrible as an army in battle array* to the devil and his followers, especially in these latter times. For Satan, knowing that he has little time† — even less than ever — to destroy souls, intensifies his efforts and his onslaughts every day. He will not hesitate to stir up savage persecutions and set treacherous snares for Mary's faithful servants and children whom he finds more difficult to overcome than others.

51. It is chiefly in reference to these last wicked persecutions of the devil, daily increasing until the advent of the reign of anti-Christ, that we should understand that first and well-known prophecy and curse of God uttered against the serpent in the garden of paradise. It is opportune to explain it here for the glory of the Blessed Virgin, the salvation of her children and the confusion of the devil. "I will place enmities between you and the woman, between your race and her race; she will crush your head and you will lie in wait for her heel". [1]

52. God has established only one enmity — but it is an irreconcilable one — which will last and even go on increasing to the end of time. That enmity is between Mary, his worthy Mother, and the devil, between the children and the servants of the Blessed Virgin and the children and followers of Lucifer.

Thus the most fearful enemy that God has set up against the devil is Mary, his holy Mother. From the time of the earthly paradise, although she existed then only in his mind, he gave her such a hatred for his accursed enemy, such ingenuity in exposing the wickedness of the ancient serpent and such power to defeat, overthrow and crush this proud rebel, that Satan fears

*Song of Songs, 6:3. † Apoc.12:12. 1 Gen.3:15.

her not only more than angels and men but in a certain sense more than God himself. This does not mean that the anger, hatred and power of God are not infinitely greater than the Blessed Virgin's, since her attributes are limited. It simply means that Satan, being so proud, suffers infinitely more in being vanquished and punished by a lowly and humble servant of God, for her humility humiliates him more than the power of God. Moreover, God has given Mary such great power over the evil spirits that, as they have often been forced unwillingly to admit through the lips of possessed persons, they fear one of her pleadings for a soul more than the prayers of all the saints, and one of her threats more than all their other torments.

53.   What Lucifer lost by pride Mary won by humility. What Eve ruined and lost by disobedience Mary saved by obedience. By obeying the serpent, Eve ruined her children as well as herself and delivered them up to him. Mary, by her perfect fidelity to God, saved her children with herself and consecrated them to his divine majesty.

54.   God has established not just one enmity but "enmities", and not only between Mary and Satan but between her race and his race. That is, God has put enmities, antipathies and hatreds between the true children of the Blessed Virgin and the children and slaves of the devil. They have no love and no sympathy for each other. The children of Belial, the slaves of Satan, the friends of the world — for they are all one and the same — have always persecuted and will persecute more than ever in the future those who belong to the Blessed Virgin, just as Cain of old persecuted his brother Abel, and Esau his brother Jacob. These are the types of the wicked and of the just. But the humble Mary will always triumph over Satan, the proud one, and so great will be her victory that she will crush his head, the very

seat of his pride. She will always unmask his serpent's cunning and expose his wicked plots. She will scatter to the winds his devilish plans and to the end of time keep her faithful servants from his cruel claws.

But Mary's power over the evil spirits will especially shine forth in the latter times, when Satan will lie in wait for her heel, that is, for her humble servants and her poor children whom she will rouse to fight against him. In the eyes of the world they will be little and poor and, like the heel, lowly in the eyes of all, downtrodden and crushed, as is the heel by the other parts of the body. But in compensation for this they will be rich in God's graces, which will be abundantly bestowed on them by Mary. They will be superior to all creatures by their great zeal and so strongly will they be supported by divine assistance that, in union with Mary, they will crush the head of Satan with their heel, that is, their humility, and bring victory to Jesus Christ.

2. Devotion to Mary especially necessary in the latter times.

55. Finally, God in these times wishes his Blessed Mother to be more known, loved and honoured than she has ever been. This will certainly come about if the elect, by the grace and light of the Holy Spirit, adopt the interior and perfect practice of the devotion which I shall later unfold. Then they will clearly see that beautiful Star of the Sea, as much as faith allows. Under her guidance they will come safely to port in spite of storms and pirates. They will perceive the splendours of this Queen and will consecrate themselves entirely to her service as subjects and slaves of love. They will experience her motherly kindness and affection for her children. They will love her tenderly and will appreciate how full of compassion she is and how much they stand in need of her help. In all circumstances they will have recourse to her as their advocate and mediatrix, with Jesus Christ. They will see clearly that she is the safest, easiest, shortest and most perfect way of approaching Jesus and will surrender themselves to her, body and soul, without reserve in order to belong entirely to Jesus.

56. But what will they be like, these servants, these slaves, these children of Mary?

They will be ministers of the Lord* who, like a flaming fire, will enkindle everywhere the fires of divine love. They will become, in Mary's powerful hands, like sharp arrows,† with which she will transfix her enemies.

They will be as the children of Levi, thoroughly purified by the fire of great tribulations and closely joined to God. [1] They will carry the gold of love in their heart, the frankincense of prayer in their mind and the myrrh of mortification in their body. They will bring to the poor and the lowly everywhere the sweet fragrance of Jesus, but they will bring the odour of death to the great, the rich and the proud of this world.

57. They will be like thunder-clouds [2] flying through the air at the slightest breath of the Holy Spirit. Attached to nothing, surprised at nothing, troubled at nothing, they will shower down the rain of God's word and of eternal life. They will thunder against sin, they will storm against the world, they will strike down the devil and his followers and for life or for death they will pierce through and through with the two-edged sword of God's word [3] all those against whom they are sent by almighty God.

58. They will be true apostles of the latter times to whom the Lord of Hosts will give eloquence and strength

* Ps.103:4;Heb.1:7.   † Ps.126:4.

1 Mal.3:3;1 Cor.6:17.   2. Isai.60:8.   3 Heb.4:12; Eph.6:17.

to work wonders and carry off glorious spoils from his enemies.* They will sleep without gold or silver and, more important still, without concern in the midst of other priests, ecclesiastics and clerics. Yet they will have the silver wings of the dove enabling them to go wherever the Holy Spirit calls them, filled as they are, with the resolve to seek the glory of God and the salvation of souls. Wherever they preach, they will leave behind them nothing but the gold of love, which is the fulfilment of the whole law.

59. Lastly, we know they will be true disciples of Jesus Christ, imitating his poverty, his humility, his contempt of the world and his love. They will point out the narrow way to God in pure truth according to the holy Gospel, and not according to the maxims of the world. Their hearts will not be troubled, nor will they show favour to anyone; they will not spare or heed or fear any man, however powerful he may be. They will have the two-edged sword of the Word of God in their mouths and the blood-stained standard of the Cross on their shoulders. They will carry the crucifix in their right hand and the rosary in their left, and the holy names of Jesus and Mary on their heart. The simplicity and self-sacrifice of Jesus will be reflected in their whole behaviour.

Such are the great men who are to come. By the will of God Mary is to prepare them to extend his rule over the impious and unbelievers. But when and how will this come about? Only God knows. For our part we must yearn and wait for it in silence and in prayer: "I have waited and waited."†

* Ps.67: 13-14   † Ps.39: 2.

CHAPTER TWO

IN WHAT DEVOTION TO MARY CONSISTS

1. Basic Principles of Devotion to Mary

60.   Having spoken briefly of the necessity of devotion to the Blessed Virgin, I must now explain what this devotion consists in. This I will do with God's help after I have laid down certain basic truths which throw light on the remarkable and sound devotion which I propose to unfold.

First Principle:
Christ must be the ultimate end of all devotions.

61.   Jesus, our Saviour, true God and true man must be the ultimate end of all our other devotions; otherwise they would be false and misleading. He is the Alpha and the Omega,* the beginning and end of everything. "We labour," says St. Paul, "only to make all men perfect in Jesus Christ."

For in him alone dwells the entire fulness of the divinity and the complete fulness of grace, virtue and perfection. In him alone we have been blessed with every spiritual blessing; he is the only teacher from whom we must learn; the only Lord on whom we should depend; the only Head to whom we should be united and the only model that we should imitate. He is the only Physician that can heal us; the only Shepherd that can feed us; the only Way that can lead us; the only Truth that we can believe; the only Life that can animate us. He alone is everything to us and he alone can satisfy all our desires.

*   Apoc.1:8.

We are given no other name under heaven by which we can be saved. God has laid no other foundation for our salvation, perfection and glory than Jesus. Every one of the faithful who is not united to him is like a branch broken from the stem of the vine. It falls and withers and is fit only to be burnt. If we live in Jesus and Jesus lives in us, we need not fear damnation. Neither angels in heaven nor men on earth, nor devils in hell, no creature whatever can harm us, for no creature can separate us from the love of God which is in Christ Jesus. Through him, with him and in him, we can do all things and render all honour and glory to the Father in the unity of the Holy Spirit; we can make ourselves perfect and be for our neighbour a fragrance of eternal life.

62. If then we are establishing sound devotion to our Blessed Lady, it is only in order to establish devotion to our Lord more perfectly, by providing a smooth but certain way of reaching Jesus Christ. If devotion to our Lady distracted us from our Lord, we would have to reject it as an illusion of the devil. But this is far from being the case. As I have already shown and will show again later on, this devotion is necessary, simply and solely because it is a way of reaching Jesus perfectly, loving him tenderly and serving him faithfully.

63. Here I turn to you for a moment, dear Jesus, to complain lovingly to your divine Majesty that the majority of Christians, and even some of the most learned among them, do not recognise the necessary bond that unites you and your Blessed Mother. Lord, you are always with Mary and Mary is always with you. She can never be without you because then she would cease to be what she is. She is so completely transformed into you by grace that she no longer lives, she no longer exists, because you alone, dear Jesus, live and reign in her more perfectly than in all the angels and saints. If we only knew the glory and the love given to you by this wonderful creature, our feelings for you and for her would be far different from those we have now. So intimately is she united to you that it would be easier to separate light from the sun, and heat from the fire. I go further, it would even be easier to separate all the angels and saints from you than Mary; for she loves you more ardently, and glorifies you more perfectly than all your other creatures put together.

64. In view of this, my dear Master, is it not astonishing and pitiful to see the ignorance and shortsightedness of men with regard to your holy Mother? I am not speaking so much of idolaters and pagans who do not know you and consequently have no knowledge of her. I am not even speaking of heretics and schismatics who have left you and your holy Church and therefore are not interested in your Mother. I am speaking of Catholics, and even of educated Catholics, who profess to teach the faith to others but do not know you or your Mother except speculatively, in a dry, cold and sterile way.

These people seldom speak of your Mother or devotion to her. They say they are afraid that devotion to her will be abused and that you will be offended by excessive honour paid to her. They protest loudly when they see or hear a devout servant of Mary speak frequently with feeling, conviction and vigour of devotion to her. When he speaks of devotion to her as a sure means of finding and loving you without fear of illusion, or when he says this devotion is a short road free from danger, or an immaculate way free from imperfection, or a wondrous secret of finding you, they put before him a thousand specious reasons to show him how wrong he is to speak so much of Mary. There are, they say, great abuses in this devotion which we should try to stamp out and we should refer people to you rather than exhort them to have devotion to your Mother, whom they already love adequately.

If they are sometimes heard speaking of devotion to your Mother, it is not for the purpose of promoting it or convincing people of it but only to destroy the abuses made of it. Yet all the while these persons are devoid of piety or genuine devotion to you, for they have no devotion to Mary. They consider the Rosary and the Scapular as devotions suitable only for simple women or ignorant people. After all, they say, we do not need them to be saved. If they come across one who loves our Lady, who says the Rosary or shows any devotion towards her, they soon move him to a change of mind and heart. They advise him to say the seven penitential psalms instead of the Rosary, and to show devotion to Jesus instead of Mary.

Dear Jesus, do these people possess your spirit? Do they please you by acting in this way? Would it please you if we were to make no effort to give pleasure to your Mother because we were afraid of offending you? Does devotion to your holy Mother hinder devotion to you? Does Mary keep for herself any honour we pay her? Is she a rival of yours? Is she a stranger having no kinship with you? Does pleasing her imply displeasing you? Does the gift of oneself to her constitute a deprivation for you? Is love for her a lessening of our love for you?

65. Nevertheless, my dear Master, the majority of learned scholars could not be further from devotion to your Mother, or show more indifference to it even if all I have just said were true. Keep me, Lord, keep me from their way of thinking and acting and let me share your feelings of gratitude, esteem, respect and love for your holy Mother. I can then love and glorify you all the more, because I will be imitating and following you more closely.

66. As though I had said nothing so far to further her honour, grant me now the grace to praise her more worthily, in spite of all her enemies who are also yours. I can then say to them boldly with the saints, "Let no one presume to expect mercy from God, who offends his holy Mother."

67. So that I may obtain from your mercy a genuine devotion to your blessed Mother and spread it throughout the whole world, help me to love you wholeheartedly, and for this intention accept this earnest prayer I offer with St. Augustine and all who truly love you.

Prayer of St. Augustine

O Jesus Christ, you are my Father, my merciful God, my great King, my good Shepherd, my only Master, my best helper, my beloved friend of overwhelming beauty, my living Bread, my eternal priest. You are my guide to my heavenly home, my one true light, my holy joy, my true way, my shining wisdom, my unfeigned simplicity, the peace and harmony of my soul, my perfect safeguard, my bounteous inheritance, my everlasting salvation.

My loving Lord, Jesus Christ, why have I ever loved or desired anything else in my life but you, my God? Where was I when I was not in communion with you? From now on, I direct all my desires to be inspired by you and centred on you. I direct them to press forward for they have tarried long enough, to hasten towards their goal, to seek the one they yearn for.

O Jesus, let him who does not love you be accursed, and filled with bitterness. O gentle Jesus, let every worthy feeling of mine show you love, take delight in you and admire you. O God of my heart and my inheritance, Christ Jesus, may my heart mellow before the influence of your spirit and may you live in me. May the flame of your love burn in my soul. May it burn incessantly on the altar of my heart. May it glow in my innermost being. May it spread its heat into the hidden recesses of my soul and on the day of my consummation may I appear before you consumed in your love.   Amen.

Second Principle: We belong to Jesus and Mary as their slaves

68.   From what Jesus Christ is in regard to us we must conclude, as St. Paul says,* that we belong not to ourselves but entirely to him as his members and his slaves, for he bought us at an infinite price — the shedding of his precious blood. Before baptism, we belonged to the devil as slaves, but baptism made us in very truth slaves of Jesus. We must therefore live, work and die for the sole purpose of bringing forth fruit for him, glorifying him in our body and letting him reign in our soul. We are his conquest, the people he has won, his heritage.†

It is for this reason that the Holy Spirit compares us: *1)* to trees which are planted along the waters of grace in the field of the Church and which must bear their fruit when the time comes; *2)* to branches of the vine of which Jesus is the stem, which must yield good grapes; *3)* to a flock of sheep of which Jesus is the Shepherd, which must increase and give milk; *4)* to good soil cultivated by God, where the seed will spread and produce crops up to thirty-fold, sixty-fold, or a hundred-fold. Our Lord cursed the barren fig-tree and condemned the slothful servant who wasted his talent.

*   Cf.1 Cor.6:20; 12:27.   † 1 Pet. 2:9.

All this proves that he wishes to receive some fruit from our wretched selves, namely, our good works, which by right belong to him alone, "created in Christ Jesus for good works".* These words of the Holy Spirit show that Jesus is the sole source and must be the sole end of all our good works, and that we must serve him not just as paid servants but as slaves of love. Let me explain what I mean.

69.   There are two ways of belonging to another person and being subject to his authority. One is by ordinary service and the other is by slavery. And so we use the terms "servant" and "slave". Ordinary service in Christian countries is when a man is employed to serve another for a certain length of time at a wage which is fixed or agreed upon. When a man is totally dependent on another for life, and must serve his master without expecting any wages or recompense, when he is treated just like a beast of the field over which the owner has the right of life and death, then it is slavery.

70.   Now there are three kinds of slavery: natural slavery, enforced slavery, and voluntary slavery. All creatures are slaves of God in the first sense, for "the earth and its fulness belong to the Lord."† The devils and the damned are slaves in the second sense. The saints in heaven and the just on earth are slaves in the third sense. Voluntary slavery is the most perfect of all three states, for by it we give the greatest glory to God, who looks into the heart and wants it to be given to him. Is he not indeed called the God of the heart or of the loving will?[1] For by this slavery we freely choose God and his service before all things, even if we were not by our very nature obliged to do so.

71.   There is a world of difference between a servant

* Eph.2:10.   † Ps.23:1.

[1] 1 Sam. 16:7; Ps.72:26.

and a slave. *1)* A servant does not give his employer all he is, all he has, and all he can acquire by himself or through others. A slave, however, gives himself to his master completely and exclusively with all he has and all he can acquire. *2)* A servant demands wages for the services rendered to his employer. A slave, on the other hand, can expect nothing, no matter what skill, attention or energy he may have put into his work. *3)* A servant can leave his employer whenever he pleases, or at least when the term of his service expires, whereas the slave has no such right. *4)* An employer has no right of life and death over a servant. Were he to kill him as he would a beast of burden, he would commit murder. But the master of a slave has by law the right of life and death over him, so that he can sell him to anyone he chooses or — if you will pardon the comparison — kill him as he would kill his horse. *5)* Finally, a servant is in his employer's service only for a time; a slave for always.

72. No other human state involves belonging more completely to another than slavery. Among Christian peoples, nothing makes a person belong more completely to Jesus and his holy Mother than voluntary slavery. Our Lord himself gave us the example of this when out of love for us he "took the form of a slave".* Our Lady gave us the same example when she called herself the handmaid or slave of the Lord. The Apostle considered it an honour to be called "slave of Christ" † Several times in Holy Scripture, Christians are referred to as "slaves of Christ". [I]

73. Granting this, I say that we must belong to Jesus and serve him not just as hired servants but as willing slaves who, moved by generous love, commit themselves to his service after the manner of slaves for the honour

* Phil.2:7.   † Rom. 1:1:·Gal.1:10.

[I] 1 Cor.7:22; 2 Tim.2:24

of belonging to him. Before we were baptised we were the slaves of the devil, but baptism made us the slaves of Jesus. Christians can only be slaves of the devil or slaves of Christ.

74. What I say in an absolute sense of our Lord, I say in a relative sense of our Blessed Lady. Jesus, in choosing her as his inseparable associate in his life, death, glory and power in heaven and on earth, has given her by grace in his kingdom all the same rights and privileges that he possesses by nature. "All that belongs to God by nature belongs to Mary by grace," say the saints, and, according to them, just as Jesus and Mary have the same will and the same power, they have also the same subjects, servants and slaves.

75. Following therefore the teaching of the saints and of many great men we can call ourselves, and become, the loving slaves of our Blessed Lady in order to become more perfect slaves of Jesus. Mary is the means our Lord chose to come to us and she is also the means we should choose to go to him, for she is not like other creatures who tend rather to lead us away from God than towards him, if we are over-attached to them. Mary's strongest inclination is to unite us to Jesus, her Son, and her Son's strongest wish is that we come to him through his Blessed Mother. He is pleased and honoured just as a king would be pleased and honoured if a citizen, wanting to become a better subject and slave of the king, made himself the slave of the queen. That is why the Fathers of the Church, and St. Bonaventure after them, assert that the Blessed Virgin is the way which leads to our Lord.

76. Moreover, if, as I have said, the Blessed Virgin is the Queen and Sovereign of heaven and earth, does she not then have as many subjects and slaves as there are creatures? "All things, including Mary herself, are subject to the power of God. All things, God included, are subject to the Virgin's power," so we are told by St. Anselm, St. Bernard, St. Bernardine and St. Bonaventure. Is it not reasonable to find that among so many slaves there should be some slaves of love, who freely choose Mary as their Queen? Should men and demons have willing slaves, and Mary have none? A king makes it a point of honour that the queen, his consort, should have her own slaves, over whom she has right of life and death, for honour and power given to the queen is honour and power given to the king. Could we possibly believe that Jesus, the best of all sons, who shared his power with his blessed Mother, would resent her having her own slaves? Has he less esteem and love for his Mother than Ahasuerus had for Esther, or Solomon for Bathsheba? Who could say or even think such a thing?

77.   But where is my pen leading me? Why am I wasting my time proving something so obvious? If people are unwilling to call themselves slaves of Mary, what does it matter? Let them become and call themselves slaves of Jesus Christ, for this is the same as being slaves of Mary, since Jesus is the fruit and glory of Mary. This is what we do perfectly in the devotion we shall discuss later.

Third Principle: We must rid ourselves of what is evil in us

78.   Our best actions are usually tainted and spoiled by the evil that is rooted in us. When pure, clear water is poured into a foul smelling jug, or wine into an unwashed cask that previously contained another wine, the clear water and the good wine are tainted and readily acquire an unpleasant odour. In the same way when God pours into our soul, infected by original and actual sin, the heavenly waters of his grace or the delicious wines of

his love, his gifts are usually spoiled and tainted by the evil sediment left in us by sin. Our actions, even those of the highest virtue, show the effects of it. It is therefore of the utmost importance that, in seeking the perfection that can be attained only by union with Jesus, we rid ourselves of all that is evil in us. Otherwise our infinitely pure Lord, who has an infinite hatred for the slightest stain in our soul, will refuse to unite us to himself and will drive us from his presence.

79. To rid ourselves of selfishness, we must first become thoroughly aware, by the light of the Holy Spirit, of our tainted nature. Of ourselves we are unable to do anything conducive to our salvation. Our human weakness is evident in everything we do and we are habitually unreliable. We do not deserve any grace from God. Our tendency to sin is always present. The sin of Adam has almost entirely spoiled and soured us, filling us with pride and corrupting every one of us, just as leaven sours, swells and corrupts the dough in which it is placed. The actual sins we have committed, whether mortal or venial, even though forgiven, have intensified our base desires, our weakness, our inconstancy and our evil tendencies, and have left a sediment of evil in our soul.

Our bodies are so corrupt that they are referred to by the Holy Spirit* as bodies of sin, as conceived and nourished in sin, and capable of any kind of sin. They are subject to a thousand ills, deteriorating from day to day and harbouring only disease, vermin and corruption.

Our soul, being united to our body, has become so carnal that it has been called flesh. "All flesh had corrupted its way."† Pride and blindness of spirit, hardness of heart, weakness and inconstancy of soul, evil inclinations, rebellious passions, ailments of the body, —

---

* Rom. 6:6; Ps.50:7.   † Gen. 6:12.

these are all we can call our own. By nature we are prouder than peacocks, we cling to the earth more than toads, we are baser than goats, more envious than serpents, greedier than pigs, fiercer than tigers, lazier than tortoises, weaker than reeds, and more changeable than weather-cocks. We have in us nothing but sin, and deserve only the wrath of God and the eternity of hell.*

80.   Is it any wonder then that our Lord laid down that anyone who aspires to be his follower must deny himself and hate his very life? He makes it clear that anyone who loves his life shall lose it and anyone who hates his life shall save it. Now, our Lord, who is infinite Wisdom, and does not give commandments without a reason, bids us hate ourselves only because we richly deserve to be hated. Nothing is more worthy of love than God and nothing is more deserving of hatred than self.

81.   Secondly, in order to empty ourselves of self, we must die daily to ourselves. This involves our renouncing what the powers of the soul and the senses of the body incline us to do. We must see as if we did not see, hear as if we did not hear and use the things of this world as if we did not use them. This is what St. Paul calls "dying daily". Unless the grain of wheat falls to the ground and dies, it remains only a single grain and does not bear any good fruit. If we do not die to self and if our holiest devotions do not lead us to this necessary and fruitful death, we shall not bear fruit of any worth and our devotions will cease to be profitable. All our good works will be tainted by self-love and self-will so that our greatest sacrifices and our best actions will be unacceptable to God. Consequently when we come to die we shall find ourselves devoid of virtue and merit and discover that we do not possess even one spark of that pure love which God shares with only those who have

* Eph. 2:3.

died to themselves and whose life is hidden with Jesus Christ in him.

82.   Thirdly, we must choose among all the devotions to the Blessed Virgin the one which will lead us most surely to this dying to self. That devotion will be the best and most sanctifying for us. For we must not believe that all that glitters is gold, all that is sweet is honey, or all that is easy to do and is done by the majority of people is the most sanctifying. Just as in nature there are secrets enabling us to do certain natural things quickly, easily and at little cost, so in the spiritual life there are secrets which enable us to perform supernatural works rapidly, smoothly and with facility Such works are, for example, emptying ourselves of self-love, filling ourselves with God, and attaining perfection.

The devotion that I propose to explain is one of these secrets of grace, for it is unknown to most Christians. Only a few devout people know of it and it is practised and appreciated by fewer still. To begin the explanation of this devotion here is a fourth truth which is a consequence of the third.

Fourth Principle: It is more humble to have an intermediary with Christ

83.   It is more perfect because it supposes greater humility to approach God through a mediator rather than directly by ourselves. Our human nature, as I have just shown, is so spoilt that if we rely on our own work, effort and preparedness to reach and please him, it is certain that our good works will be tainted and carry little weight with him. They will not induce him to unite himself to us or answer our prayers. God has his reasons for giving us mediators with him. He saw our unworthiness and helplessness and had pity on us. To give us access to his mercies he provided us with powerful advocates, so that to neglect these mediators and to approach his infinite holiness directly and without help from any one of them, is to be lacking in humility and respect towards God who is so great and so holy. It would mean that we have less esteem for the King of kings than for an earthly king or ruler, for we would not dare approach an earthly king without a friend to speak for us.

84. Our Lord is our Advocate and our Mediator of redemption with God the Father. It is through him that we must pray with the whole Church, triumphant and militant. It is through him that we have access to God the Father. We should never appear before God, our Father, unless we are supported by the merits of his Son, and, so to speak, clothed in them, as young Jacob was clothed in the skin of the young goats when he appeared before his father Isaac to receive his blessing.

85. But have we no need at all of a mediator with the Mediator himself? Are we pure enough to be united directly to Christ without any help? Is Jesus not God, equal in every way to the Father? Therefore is he not the Holy of Holies, having a right to the same respect as his Father? If in his infinite love he became our security and our Mediator with his Father, whom he wished to appease in order to redeem us from our debts, should we on that account show him less respect and have less regard for the majesty and holiness of his person?

Let us not be afraid to say with St. Bernard that we need a mediator with the Mediator himself and the divinely-honoured Mary is the one most able to fulfil this office of love. Through her, Jesus came to us; through her, we should go to him. If we are afraid of going directly to Jesus, who is God, because of his infinite greatness, or our lowliness, or our sins, let us implore without fear the help and intercession of Mary, our Mother. She is kind, she is tender, and there is nothing harsh or forbidding about her, nothing too sublime or too brilliant. When we see her, we see but our own human nature. She is not the sun, dazzling our weak sight by the brightness of its rays. Rather, she is fair and gentle as the moon, which receives its light from the sun and softens it and adapts it to our limited perception.

She is so full of love that no one who asks for her intercession is rejected, no matter how sinful he may be. The saints say that it never has been known since the world began that anyone had recourse to our blessed Lady, with trust and perseverance, and was rejected. Her power is so great that her prayers are never refused. She has but to appear in prayer before her Son and he at once welcomes her and grants her requests. He is always lovingly conquered by the prayers of the dear Mother who bore him and nourished him.

86.   All this is taken from St. Bernard and St. Bonaventure. According to them, we have three steps to take in order to reach God. The first, nearest to us and most suited to our capacity, is Mary; the second is Jesus Christ; the third is God the Father. To go to Jesus, we should go to Mary, our mediatrix of intercession. To go to God the Father, we must go to Jesus, our Mediator of Redemption. This order is perfectly observed in the devotion I shall speak about further on.

Fifth Principle: It is difficult to keep the graces received from God

87.   It is very difficult, considering our weakness and frailty, to keep the graces and treasures we have received from God.

1) We carry this treasure which is worth more than heaven and earth, in fragile vessels,* that is, in a corruptible body and in a weak and wavering soul which requires very little to depress and disturb it.

88. *2)* The evil spirits, cunning thieves that they are, can take us by surprise and rob us of all we possess. They are watching day and night for the right moment. They roam about incessantly seeking to devour us† and to snatch from us in one brief moment of sin all the grace and merit we have taken years to acquire. Their malice and their experience, their cunning and their numbers ought to make us ever fearful of such a misfortune happening to us. People richer in grace and virtue, more experienced and advanced in holiness than we are, have been caught off their guard and robbed and stripped of everything. How many cedars of Lebanon, how many stars of the firmament have we sadly watched fall and lose in a short time their loftiness and their brightness!

What has brought about this unexpected reverse? Not the lack of grace, for this is denied no one. It was a lack of humility; they considered themselves well able to hold on to their treasures. They believed their house secure enough and their coffers strong enough to safeguard their precious treasure of grace. It was because of their unconscious reliance on self — although it seemed to them that they were relying solely on the grace of God — that the most just Lord left them to themselves and allowed them to be despoiled. If they had only known of the wonderful devotion that I shall later explain, they would have entrusted their treasure to Mary, the powerful and faithful Virgin. She would have kept it for them as if it were her own possession and even have considered that trust an obligation of justice.

*2 Cor.4:7.   † 1 Pet.5:8.

89.   *3)* It is difficult to persevere in holiness because of the excessive corrupting influence of the world. The world is so corrupt that it seems almost inevitable that religious hearts be soiled, if not by its mud, at least by its dust. It is something of a miracle for anyone to stand firm in the midst of this raging torrent and not be swept away; to weather this stormy sea and not be drowned, or robbed by pirates; to breathe this pestilential air and not be contaminated by it. It is Mary, the singularly faithful Virgin over whom Satan had never any power, who works this miracle for those who truly love her.

2. Marks of false and authentic devotion to Mary

90.   Now that we have established these five basic truths, it is all the more necessary to make the right choice of the true devotion to our blessed Lady, for now more than ever there are false devotions to her which can easily be mistaken for true ones. The devil, like a counterfeiter and crafty, experienced deceiver, has already misled and ruined many Christians by means of fraudulent devotions to our Lady. Day by day he uses his diabolical experience to lead many more to their doom, fooling them, lulling them to sleep in sin and assuring them that a few prayers, even badly said, and a few exterior practices inspired by himself, are authentic devotions. A counterfeiter usually makes coins only of gold and silver, rarely of other metals, because these latter would not be worth the trouble. Similarly, the devil leaves other devotions alone and counterfeits mostly those directed to Jesus and Mary, as for example, devotion to the Holy Eucharist and to the Blessed Virgin, because these are to other devotions what gold and silver are to other metals.

91. It is therefore very important, first, to recognise false devotions to our Blessed Lady so as to avoid them, and to recognise true devotion in order to practise it. Second, among so many different forms of true devotion to our Blessed Lady we should choose the one most perfect and the most pleasing to her, the one that gives greater glory to God and is most sanctifying for us.

1) *False devotion to our Lady*

92. There are, I find, seven kinds of false devotion to Mary, namely, the devotion of (1) the critical, (2) the scrupulous, (3) the superficial, (4) the presumptuous, (5) the inconstant, (6) the hypocritical, (7) the self-interested.

93. *Critical* devotees are for the most part proud scholars, people of independent and self-satisfied minds, who deep down in their hearts have a vague sort of devotion to Mary. However, they criticise nearly all those forms of devotion to her which simple and pious people use to honour their good Mother just because such practices do not appeal to them. They question all miracles and stories which testify to the mercy and power of the blessed Virgin, even those recorded by trustworthy authors or taken from the chronicles of religious orders. They cannot bear to see simple and humble people on their knees before an altar or statue of our Lady, or at prayer before some outdoor shrine. They even accuse them of idolatry as if they were adoring the wood or the stone. They say that as far as they are concerned they do not care for such outward display of devotions and that they are not so gullible as to believe all the fairy tales and stories told of our blessed Lady. When you tell them how admirably the Fathers of the Church praised our Lady, they reply that the Fathers exaggerated as orators do, or that their words are misrepresented. These false devotees, these proud worldly people are greatly to be feared. They do untold harm to devotion to our Lady. While pretending to correct abuses, they succeed only too well in turning people away from this devotion.

94.   *Scrupulous* devotees are those who imagine they are slighting the Son by honouring the Mother. They fear that by exalting Mary they are belittling Jesus. They cannot bear to see people giving to our Lady the praises due to her and which the Fathers of the Church have lavished upon her. It annoys them to see more people kneeling before Mary's altar than before the Blessed Sacrament, as if these acts were at variance with each other, or as if those who were praying to our Lady were not praying through her to Jesus. They do not want us to speak too often of her or to pray so often to her.

Here are some of the things they say: "What is the good of all these rosaries, confraternities and exterior devotions to our Lady? There is a great deal of ignorance in all this. It is making a mockery of religion. Tell us about those who are devoted to Jesus (and they often pronounce his name without uncovering their heads). We should go directly to Jesus since he is our sole Mediator. We must preach Jesus; that is sound devotion." There is some truth in what they say, but the inference they draw to prevent devotion to our Lady is very insidious. It is a subtle snare of the evil one under the pretext of promoting a greater good. For we never give more honour to Jesus than when we honour his Mother, and we honour her simply and solely to honour him all the more perfectly. We go to her only as a way leading to the goal we seek — Jesus, her Son.

95. The Church, with the Holy Spirit, blesses our Lady first, then Jesus, "Blessed art thou among women and blessed is the fruit of thy womb, Jesus." Not that Mary is greater than Jesus, or even equal to him — that would be an intolerable heresy. But in order to bless Jesus more perfectly we should first bless Mary. Let us say with all those truly devoted to her, despite these false and scrupulous devotees, "O Mary, blessed art thou among women and blessed is the fruit of thy womb, Jesus."

96. *Superficial* devotees are people whose entire devotion to our Lady consists in exterior practices. Only the externals of devotion appeal to them because they have no interior spirit. They say many rosaries with great haste and assist at many Masses distractedly. They take part in processions of our Lady without inner fervour. They join her confraternities without reforming their lives or restraining their passions or imitating Mary's virtues. All that appeals to them is the emotional aspect of this devotion, but the substance of it has no appeal at all. If they do not *feel* a warmth in their devotions, they think they are doing nothing; they become upset, and give up everything, or else do things only when they feel like it. The world is full of these shallow devotees, and there are none more critical of men of prayer who regard the interior devotion as the essential aspect and strive to acquire it, without, however, neglecting a reasonable external expression which always accompanies true devotion.

97. *Presumptuous* devotees are sinners who give full rein to their passions or their love of the world, and who, under the fair name of Christian and servant of our Lady, conceal pride, avarice, lust, drunkenness, anger, swearing, slandering, injustice and other vices. They sleep peacefully in their wicked habits, without making any great effort to correct them, believing that their devotion to our Lady gives them this sort of liberty. They convince themselves that God will forgive them, that they will not die without confession, that they will not be lost for all eternity. They take all this for granted because they say the Rosary, fast on Saturdays, are enrolled in the Confraternity of the Holy Rosary or the Scapular, or a sodality of our Lady, wear the medal or the little chain of our Lady.

When you tell them that such a devotion is only an illusion of the devil and a dangerous presumption which may well ruin them, they refuse to believe you. God is good and merciful, they reply, and he has not made us to damn us. No man is without sin. We will not die without confession, and a good act of contrition at death is all that is needed. Moreover, they say they have devotion to our Lady; that they wear the scapular; that they recite faithfully and humbly every day the seven Our Fathers and seven Hail Marys in her honour; that sometimes they even say the Rosary and the Office of our Lady, as well as fasting and performing other good works.

Blinding themselves still more, they quote stories they have heard or read — whether true or false does not bother them — which relate how people who had died in mortal sin were brought back to life again to go to confession, or how their soul was miraculously retained in their bodies until confession, because in their lifetime they said a few prayers, or performed a few pious acts, in honour of our Lady. Others are supposed to have obtained from God at the moment of death, through the merciful intercession of the Blessed Virgin, sorrow and pardon for their sins, and so were saved. Accordingly, these people expect the same thing to happen to them.

98.   Nothing in our Christian religion is so deserving
of condemnation as this diabolical presumption. How
can we truthfully claim to love and honour the Blessed
Virgin when by our sins we pitilessly wound, pierce,
crucify and outrage her Son? If Mary made it a rule to
save by her mercy this sort of person, she would be
condoning wickedness and helping to outrage and crucify her Son. Who would even dare to think of such a
thing?

99.   I declare that such an abuse of devotion to her
is a horrible sacrilege and, next to an unworthy
Communion, is the greatest and the least pardonable
sin, because devotion to our Lady is the holiest and
best after devotion to the Blessed Sacrament.

      I admit that to be truly devoted to our Lady, it
is not absolutely necessary to be so holy as to avoid
all sin, although this is desirable. But at least it is necessary (note what I am going to say), *(i)* to be genuinely
determined to avoid at least all mortal sin, which out-
rages the Mother as well as the Son; *(ii)* to practise
great self-restraint in order to avoid sin; *(iii)* to join her
confraternities, say the Rosary or other prayers, fast on
Saturdays, and so on.

100.   Such means are surprisingly effective in converting even the hardened sinner. Should you be such a
sinner, with one foot in the abyss, I advise you to do as
I have said. But there is an essential condition. You
must perform these good works solely to obtain from
God, through the intercession of our Lady, the grace to
regret your sins, obtain pardon for them and overcome
your evil habits, and not live complacently in the state
of sin, disregarding the warning voice of conscience,
the example of our Lord and the saints, and the teaching of the holy gospel.

101.   *Inconstant* devotees are those whose devotion to our Lady is practised in fits and starts. Sometimes they are fervent and sometimes they are luke-warm. Sometimes they appear ready to do anything to please our Lady, and then shortly afterwards they have completely changed. They start by embracing every devotion to our Lady. They join her confraternities, but they do not faithfully observe the rules. They are as changeable as the moon, and like the moon Mary puts them under her feet.* Because of their fickleness they are unworthy to be included among the servants of the Virgin most faithful, because faithfulness and constancy are the hallmarks of Mary's servants. It is better not to burden ourselves with a multitude of prayers and pious practices but rather adopt only a few and perform them with love and perseverance in spite of opposition from the devil the world and the flesh.

102. There is another category of false devotees of our Lady, — *hypocritical* ones. These hide their sins and evil habits under the mantle of the Blessed Virgin so as to appear to their fellow-men different from what they are.

103. Then there are the *self-interested* devotees who turn to her only to win a court-case, to escape some danger, to be cured of some ailment, or have some similar need satisfied. Except when in need they never think of her. Such people are acceptable neither to God nor to his Mother.

104. We must, then, carefully avoid joining the *critical* devotees, who believe nothing and find fault with everything; the *scrupulous* ones who, out of respect for our Lord, are afraid of having too much devotion to his Mother; the *exterior* devotees whose devotion consists entirely in outward practices; the *presumptuous* devotees who under cover of a fictitious devotion to our Lady wallow in their sins; the *in-*

* Ecclus. 27:12; Apoc. 12:1.

constant devotees who, being unstable, change their devotional practices or abandon them altogether at the slightest temptation; the *hypocritical* ones who join confraternities and wear emblems of our Lady only to be thought of as good people; finally, the *self-interested* devotees who pray to our Lady only to be rid of bodily ills or to obtain material benefits.

2) Marks of authentic devotion to our Lady

105. After having explained and condemned false devotions to the Blessed Virgin we shall now briefly describe what true devotion is. It is *interior, trustful, holy, constant,* and *disinterested.*

106. *First, true devotion to our Lady is interior,* that is, it comes from within the mind and the heart and follows from the esteem in which we hold her, the high regard we have for her greatness, and the love we bear her.

107. *Second, it is trustful,* that is to say, it fills us with confidence in the Blessed Virgin, the confidence that a child has for its loving Mother. It prompts us to go to her in every need of body and soul with great simplicity, trust and affection. We implore our Mother's help always, everywhere, and for everything. We pray to her to be enlightened in our doubts, to be put back on the right path when we go astray, to be protected when we are tempted, to be strengthened when we are weakening, to be lifted up when we fall into sin, to be encouraged when we are losing heart, to be rid of our scruples, to be consoled in the trials, crosses and disappointments of life. Finally, in all our afflictions of body and soul, we naturally turn to Mary for help, with never a fear of importuning her or displeasing our Lord.

108. *Third, true devotion to our Lady is holy,* that is, it leads us to avoid sin and to imitate the virtues of Mary. Her ten principal virtues are: deep humility, lively faith, blind obedience, unceasing prayer, constant self-denial, surpassing purity, ardent love, heroic patience, angelic kindness, and heavenly wisdom.

109. *Fourth, true devotion to our Lady is constant.* It strengthens us in our desire to do good and prevents us from giving up our devotional practices too easily. It gives us the courage to oppose the fashions and maxims of the world, the vexations and unruly inclinations of the flesh and the temptations of the devil. Thus a person truly devoted to our Blessed Lady is not changeable, fretful, scrupulous or timid. We do not say however that such a person never sins or that his sensible feelings of devotion never change. When he has fallen, he stretches out his hand to his Blessed Mother and rises again. If he loses all taste and feeling for devotion, he is not at all upset because a good and faithful servant of Mary is guided in his life by faith in Jesus and Mary, and not by feelings.

110. *Fifth, true devotion to Mary is disinterested.* It inspires us to seek God in his Blessed Mother and not ourselves. The true subject of Mary does not serve his illustrious Queen for selfish gain. He does not serve her for temporal or eternal well-being but simply and solely because she has the right to be served and God alone in her. He loves her not so much because she is good to him or because he expects something from her, but simply because she is lovable. That is why he loves and serves her just as faithfully in weariness and dryness of soul as in sweet and sensible fervour. He loves her as much on Calvary as at Cana. How pleasing and precious in the sight of God and his holy Mother must these servants of Mary be, who serve her without any self-seeking. How rare they are nowadays! It is to increase their number that I have taken up my pen to write down what I have been teaching with success both publicly and in private in my missions for many years.

111. I have already said many things about the Blessed Virgin and, as I am trying to fashion a true servant of Mary and a true disciple of Jesus, I have still a great deal to say, although through ignorance, inability, and lack of time, I shall leave infinitely more unsaid.

112. But my labour will be well rewarded if this little book falls into the hands of a noble soul, a child of God and of Mary, born not of blood nor the will of the flesh nor of the will of man. My time will be well spent if, by the grace of the Holy Spirit, after having read this book he is convinced of the supreme value of the solid devotion to Mary I am about to describe. If I thought that my guilty blood could help the reader to accept in his heart the truths that I set down in honour of my dear Mother and Queen, I, her most unworthy child and slave, would use it instead of ink to write these words. I would hope to find faithful souls who, by their perseverance in the devotion I teach, will repay her for the loss she has suffered through my ingratitude and infidelity.

113. I feel more than ever inspired to believe and expect the complete fulfilment of the desire that is deeply engraved on my heart and what I have prayed to God for over many years, namely, that in the near or distant future the Blessed Virgin will have more children, servants and slaves of love than ever before, and that through them Jesus, my dear Lord, will reign more than ever in the hearts of men.

114. I clearly foresee that raging beasts will come in

fury to tear to pieces with their diabolical teeth this little book and the one the Holy Spirit made use of to write it, or they will cause it at least to lie hidden in the darkness and silence of a chest and so prevent it from seeing the light of day.* They will even attack and persecute those who read it and put into practice what it contains. But no matter! So much the better! It even gives me encouragement to hope for great success at the prospect of a mighty legion of brave and valiant soldiers of Jesus and Mary, both men and women, who will fight the devil, the world, and corrupt nature in the perilous times that are sure to come.

"Let the reader understand. Let him accept this teaching who can".†

3) Principal practices of devotion to Our Lady

115. There are several *interior* practices of true devotion to the Blessed Virgin. Here briefly are the main ones:

(1) Honouring her, as the worthy Mother of God, by the cult of hyperdulia, that is, esteeming and honouring her more than all the other saints as the masterpiece of grace and the foremost in holiness after Jesus Christ, true God and true man.

(2) Meditating on her virtues, her privileges and her actions.

(3) Contemplating her sublime dignity.

(4) Offering to her acts of love, praise and gratitude.

(5) Invoking her with a joyful heart.

(6) Offering ourselves to her and uniting ourselves to her.

(7) Doing everything to please her.

*This prediction was literally fulfilled. The manuscript of the book was hidden away in a chest during the French Revolution. It was discovered in 1842 and published for the first time in 1843.
† Mt. 24: 15; 19:12 .

(8) Beginning, carrying out and completing our actions through her, in her, with her and for her in order to do them through Jesus, in Jesus, with Jesus, and for Jesus, our last end. We shall explain this last practice later.

116. True devotion to our Lady has also several *exterior* practices. Here are the principal ones:

(1) Enrolling in her confraternities and joining her sodalities.

(2) Joining religious orders dedicated to her.

(3) Making her privileges known and appreciated.

(4) Giving alms, fasting, performing interior and exterior acts of self-denial in her honour.

(5) Carrying such signs of devotion to her as the rosary, the scapular or a little chain.

(6) Reciting with attention, devotion and reverence the fifteen decades of the Rosary in honour of the fifteen principal mysteries of our Lord, or at least five decades in honour of the Joyful mysteries — the Annunciation, the Visitation, the Birth of our Lord, the Purification, the Finding of the Child Jesus in the Temple; or the Sorrowful mysteries: the Agony in the Garden, the Scourging, the Crowning with thorns, the Carrying of the Cross, and the Crucifixion; or the Glorious mysteries: the Resurrection of our Lord, the Ascension, the Descent of the Holy Spirit, the Assumption of our Lady, body and soul, into heaven, the Crowning of Mary by the Blessed Trinity.

One may also choose any of the following prayers: the Rosary of six or seven decades in honour of the years our Lady is believed to have spent on earth; the Little Crown of the Blessed Virgin, composed of three Our Fathers and twelve Hail Marys in honour of her crown of twelve stars or privileges; the Little Office of our Lady so widely accepted and recited in the Church; the Little Psalter of the Blessed Virgin, composed in her honour by St. Bonaventure, which is so heart-warming and so devotional that you cannot recite it without being moved by it; the fourteen Our Fathers and Hail Marys in honour of her fourteen joys. There are various other prayers and hymns of the Church, such as the hymns of the liturgical seasons, the *Ave Maris Stella,* the *O Gloriosa Domina;* the *Magnificat* and other prayers which are found in all prayer-books.

(7) Singing hymns to her or teaching others to sing them.

(8) Genuflecting or bowing to her each morning while saying for example sixty or a hundred times, "Hail Mary, Virgin most faithful", so that through her intercession with God we may faithfully correspond with his graces throughout the day; and in the evening saying "Hail Mary, Mother of Mercy", asking her to obtain God's pardon for the sins we have committed during the day.

(9) Taking charge of her confraternities, decorating her altars, crowning and adorning her statues.

(10) Carrying her statues or having others carry them in procession, or keeping a small one on one's person as an effective protection against the evil one.

(11) Having statues made of her, or her name engraved and placed on the walls of churches or houses and on the gates and entrances of towns, churches and houses.

(12) Solemnly giving oneself to her by a special consecration.

117. The Holy Spirit has inspired saintly souls with many other practices of true devotion to the Blessed Virgin, all of which are conducive to holiness. You can read of them in detail in *Paradise opened to Philagia,* a collection of many devotions practised by holy people to honour the Blessed Vírgin, compiled by Fr. Paul Barry of the Society of Jesus. These devotions are a wonderful help for souls seeking holiness provided they are performed in a worthy manner, that is:

(1) With the right intention of pleasing God alone, seeking union with Jesus, our last end, and giving edification to our neighbour.

(2) With attention, avoiding wilful distractions.

(3) With devotion, avoiding haste and negligence.

(4) With decorum and respectful bodily posture.

4) The Perfect Practice

118. Having read nearly every book on devotion to the Blessed Virgin and talked to the most saintly and learned people of the day, I can now state with conviction that I have never known or heard of any devotion to our Lady which is comparable to the one I am going to speak of. No other devotion calls for more sacrifices for God, none empties us more completely of self and self-love, none keeps us more firmly in the grace of God and the grace of God in us. No other devotion unites us more perfectly and more easily to Jesus. Finally no devotion gives more glory to God, is more sanctifying for ourselves or more helpful to our neighbour.

119. As this devotion essentially consists in a state of soul, it will not be understood in the same way by everyone. Some — the great majority — will stop short at the threshold and go no further. Others — not many — will take but one step into its interior. Who will take a second step? Who will take a third? Finally who will remain in it permanently? Only the one to whom the Spirit of Jesus reveals the secret. The Holy Spirit himself will lead this faithful soul from strength to strength, from grace to grace, from light to light, until he attains transformation into Jesus in the fulness of his age on earth and of his glory in heaven.

PART II

THE PERFECT DEVOTION TO OUR LADY

CHAPTER THREE

THE PERFECT CONSECRATION TO JESUS CHRIST

1. A complete consecration to Mary

120. As all perfection consists in our being conformed, united and consecrated to Jesus it naturally follows that the most perfect of all devotions is that which conforms, unites, and consecrates us most completely to Jesus. Now of all God's creatures Mary is the most conformed to Jesus. It therefore follows that, of all devotions, devotion to her makes for the most effective consecration and conformity to him. The more one is consecrated to Mary, the more one is consecrated to Jesus.

That is why perfect consecration to Jesus is but a perfect and complete consecration of oneself to the Blessed Virgin, which is the devotion I teach; or in other words, it is the perfect renewal of the vows and promises of holy baptism.

121. This devotion consists in giving oneself entirely to Mary in order to belong entirely to Jesus through her. It requires us to give:

(1) Our body with its senses and members;

(2) Our soul with its faculties;

(3) Our present material possessions and all we shall acquire in the future;

(4) Our interior and spiritual possessions, that is, our merits, virtues and good actions of the past, the present and the future.

In other words, we give her all that we possess both in our natural life and in our spiritual life, as well as everything we shall acquire in the future in the order of nature, of grace, and of glory in heaven. This we do without any reservation, not even of a penny, a hair, or the smallest good deed. And we give for all eternity without claiming or expecting, in return for our offering and our service, any other reward than the honour of belonging to our Lord through Mary and in Mary, even though our Mother were not — as in fact she always is — the most generous and appreciative of all God's creatures.

122. Note here that two things must be considered regarding our good works, namely, satisfaction and merit or, in other words, their satisfactory or prayer value and their meritorious value. The satisfactory or prayer value of a good work is the good action in so far as it makes condign atonement for the punishment due to sin or obtains some new grace. The meritorious value or merit is the good action in so far as it merits grace and eternal glory. Now by this consecration of ourselves to the Blessed Virgin we give her all satisfactory and prayer value as well as the meritorious value of our good works, in other words, all the satisfactions and the merits. We give her our merits, graces and virtues, not that she might give them to others, for they are, strictly speaking, not transferable, because Jesus alone, in making himself our surety with his Father, had the power to impart his merits to us. But we give them to her that she may keep, increase and embellish them for us, as we shall explain later, and we give her our acts of atonement that she may apply them where she pleases for God's greater glory.

123. It follows then: 1) that by this devotion we give to Jesus all we can possibly give him, and in the most perfect manner, that is, through Mary's hands. Indeed we give him far more than we do by other devotions which require us to give only part of our time some of our good works or acts of atonement and penances. In this devotion everything is given and consecrated, even the right to dispose freely of one's spiritual goods and the satisfactions earned by daily good works. This is not done even in religious orders. Members of religious orders give God their earthly goods by the vow of poverty, the goods of the body by the vow of chastity, their free will by the vow of obedience, and sometimes their freedom of movement by the vow of enclosure. But they do not give him by these vows the liberty and right to dispose of the value of their good works. They do not despoil themselves of what a Christian considers most precious and most dear — his merits and satisfactions.

124. 2) It follows then that anyone who in this way consecrates and sacrifices himself voluntarily to Jesus through Mary may no longer dispose of the value of any of his good actions. All his sufferings, all his thoughts, words, and deeds belong to Mary. She can then dispose of them in accordance with the will of her Son and for his greater glory. This dependence, however, is without detriment to the duties of a person's present and future state of life. One such duty, for example, would be that of a priest who, by virtue of his office or otherwise, must apply the satisfactory or prayer value of the Mass to a particular person. For this consecration can only be made in accordance with the order established by God and in keeping with the duties of one's state of life.

125. 3) It follows that we consecrate ourselves at one and the same time to Mary and to Jesus. We give ourselves to Mary because Jesus chose her as the perfect means to unite himself to us and unite us to him. We give ourselves to Jesus because he is our last end. Since he is our Redeemer and our God we are indebted to him for all that we are.

2. A perfect renewal of baptismal promises

126. I have said that this devotion could rightly be called a perfect renewal of the vows and promises of holy baptism. Before baptism every Christian was a slave of the devil because he belonged to him. At baptism he has either personally or through his sponsors solemnly renounced Satan, his seductions and his works. He has chosen Jesus as his Master and sovereign Lord and undertaken to depend upon him as a slave of love. This is what is done in the devotion I am presenting to you. We renounce the devil, the world, sin and self, as expressed in the act of consecration, and we give ourselves entirely to Jesus through Mary. We even do something more than at baptism, when ordinarily our god-parents speak for us and we are given to Jesus only by proxy. In this devotion we give ourselves personally and freely and we are fully aware of what we are doing.

In holy baptism we do not give ourselves to Jesus explicitly through Mary, nor do we give him the value of our good actions. After baptism we remain entirely free either to apply that value to anyone we wish or keep it for ourselves. But by this consecration we give ourselves explicitly to Jesus through Mary's hands and we include in our consecration the value of all our actions.

127. "Men" says St. Thomas, "vow in baptism to renounce the devil and all his seductions." "This vow," says St. Augustine, "is the greatest and the most indispensable of all vows." Canon Law experts say the same thing: "The vow we make at baptism is the most important of all vows." But does anyone keep this great vow? Does anyone fulfil the promises of baptism faithfully? Is it not true that nearly all Christians prove unfaithful to the promises made to Jesus in baptism? Where does this universal failure come from, if not from man's habitual forgetfulness of the promises and responsibilities of baptism and from the fact that scarcely anyone makes a personal ratification of the contract made with God through his sponsors?

128. This is so true that the Council of Sens, convened by order of the Emperor Louis the Debonair to remedy the grave disorders of Christendom, came to the conclusion that the main cause of this moral breakdown was man's forgetfulness of his baptismal obligations and his disregard for them. It could suggest no better way of remedying this great evil than to encourage all Christians to renew the promises and vows of baptism.

129. The Catechism of the Council of Trent, faithful interpreter of that holy Council, exhorts priests to do the same and to encourage the faithful to remember and to hold fast to the belief that they are bound and consecrated as slaves to Jesus, their Redeemer and Lord. "The parish priest shall exhort the faithful never to lose sight of the fact that they are bound in conscience to dedicate and consecrate themselves for ever to their Lord and Redeemer as his slaves."

130. Now the Councils, the Fathers of the Church and experience itself, all indicate that the best remedy for the frequent lapses of Christians is to remind them of the responsibilities of their baptism and have them renew the vows they made at that time. Is it not reasonable therefore to do this in our day and in a perfect manner by adopting this devotion with its consecration to our Lord through his Blessed Mother? I say, "in a perfect manner," for in making this consecration to Jesus we are adopting the perfect means of giving ourselves to him, which is the most Blessed Virgin Mary.

131. No one can object that this devotion is novel

or of no value. It is not new, since the Councils, the Fathers of the Church, and many authors both past and present, speak of consecration to our Lord or renewal of baptismal vows as something going back to ancient times and recommended to all the faithful. Nor is it valueless, since the chief source of moral disorders and the consequent eternal loss of Christians spring from forgetfulness of this practice and indifference to it.

132. Some may object that this devotion makes us powerless to help the souls of our relatives, friends and benefactors, since it requires us to give our Lord, through Mary, the value of our good works, prayers, penances, and alms-giving.

To them I reply: 1) It is inconceivable that our friends, relatives and benefactors should suffer any loss because we have dedicated and consecrated ourselves unconditionally to the service of Jesus and Mary; it would be an affront to the power and goodness of Jesus and Mary who will surely come to the aid of our relatives, friends and benefactors whether from our meagre spiritual assets or from other sources.

2) This devotion does not prevent us from praying for others, both the living and the dead, even though the application of our good works depends on the will of our Blessed Lady. On the contrary, it will make us pray with even greater confidence. Imagine a rich man, who, wanting to show his esteem for a great prince, gives his entire fortune to him. Would not that man have greater confidence in asking the prince to help one of his friends who needs assistance? Indeed the prince would only be too happy to have such an opportunity of proving his gratitude to one who had sacrificed all that he possessed to enrich him, thereby impoverishing himself to do him honour. The same must be said of our Lord and our Lady. They will never allow them-

selves to be outdone in gratitude.

133. Some may say, perhaps, if I give our Lady the full value of my actions to apply it to whom she wills, I may have to suffer a long time in purgatory. This objection, which arises from self-love and from an unawareness of the generosity of God and his holy Mother, refutes itself.

Take a fervent and generous soul who values God's interests more than his own. He gives God all he has without reserve till he can give no more. He desires only that the glory and the kingdom of Jesus may come through his Mother, and he does all he can to bring this about. Will this generous and unselfish soul, I ask, be punished more in the next world for having been more generous and unselfish than other people? Far from it! For we shall see later that our Lord and his Mother will prove most generous to such a soul with gifts of nature, grace and glory in this life and in the next.

134. We must now consider as briefly as possible: 1) The *motives* which commend this devotion to us, 2) the wonderful *effects* it produces in faithful souls, and 3) the *practices* of this devotion.

CHAPTER FOUR

MOTIVES WHICH RECOMMEND THIS DEVOTION

1. By it we give ourselves completely to God

135. This first motive shows us the excellence of the consecration of ourselves to Jesus through Mary.

We can conceive of no higher calling than that of being in the service of God and we believe that the least of God's servants is richer, stronger and nobler than any earthly monarch who does not serve God. How rich and strong and noble then must the good and faithful servant be, who serves God as unreservedly and as completely as he possibly can! Just such a person is the faithful and loving slave of Jesus and Mary. He has indeed surrendered himself entirely to the service of the King of kings through Mary, his Mother, keeping nothing for himself. All the gold of the world and the beauties of the heavens could not recompense him for what he has done.

136. Other congregations, associations and confraternities set up in honour of our Lord and our Blessed Lady, which do so much good in the Church, do not require their members to give up absolutely everything. They simply prescribe for them the performance of certain acts and practices in fulfilment of their obligations. They leave them free to dispose of the rest of their actions as well as their time. But this devotion makes us give Jesus and Mary all our thoughts, words, actions, and sufferings and every moment of our lives without exception. Thus, whatever we do, whether we are awake or asleep, whether we eat or drink, whether we do important or unimportant work, it will always be true to say that everything is done for Jesus and Mary. Our offering always holds good, whether we think of it or not, unless we explicitly retract it. How consoling this is!

137. Moreover, as I have said before, no other act of devotion enables us to rid ourselves so easily of the possessiveness which slips unnoticed even into our best actions. This is a remarkable grace which our dear Lord grants us in return for the heroic and selfless surrender to him through Mary of the entire value of our good works. If even in this life he gives a hundredfold reward to those who renounce all material, temporal and perishable things out of love for him, how generously will he reward those who give up even interior and spiritual goods for his sake!

138. Jesus, our dearest friend, gave himself to us without reserve, body and soul, graces and merits. As St. Bernard says, "He won me over entirely by giving himself entirely to me." Does not simple justice as well as gratitude require that we give him all we possibly can? He was generous with us first, so let us be generous to him in return and he will prove still more generous to us during life, at the hour of death, and throughout eternity. "He will be generous towards the generous."

2. It helps us to imitate Christ

139. Our good Master stooped to enclose himself in the womb of the Blessed Virgin, a captive and loving slave, and to make himself subject to her for thirty years. As I said earlier, the human mind is bewildered when it reflects seriously upon this conduct of Incarnate Wisdom. He did not choose to give himself in a direct manner to the human race though he could easily have done so. He chose to come through the Virgin Mary. Thus he did not come into the world independently of others in the flower of his manhood, but he came as a frail little child dependent on the care and attention of his Mother. Consumed with the desire to give glory to God, his Father, and save the human race, he saw no better or shorter way to do so than by submitting completely to Mary.

He did this not just for the first eight, ten or fifteen years of his life like other children, but for thirty years. He gave more glory to God, his Father, during all those years of submission and dependence than he would have given by spending them working miracles, preaching far and wide, and converting all mankind. Otherwise he would have done all these things.

What immeasurable glory then do we give to God when, following the example of Jesus, we submit to Mary! With such a convincing and well-known example before us, can we be so foolish as to believe that there is a better and shorter way of giving God glory than by submitting ourselves to Mary, as Jesus did?

140. Let me remind you again of the dependence shown by the three divine Persons on our Blessed Lady. Theirs is the example which fully justifies our dependence on her. The Father gave and still gives his Son only through her. He raises children for himself only through her. He dispenses his graces to us only through her. God the Son was prepared for mankind in general by her alone. Mary, in union with the Holy Spirit, still conceives him and brings him forth daily. It is through her alone that the Son distributes his merits and virtues. The Holy Spirit formed Jesus only through her, and he forms the members of the Mystical Body and dispenses his gifts and his favours through her.

With such a compelling example of the three divine Persons before us, we would be extremely perverse to ignore her and not consecrate ourselves to her.

Indeed we would be blind if we did not see the need for Mary in approaching God and making our total offering to him.

141. Here are a few passages from the Fathers of the Church which I have chosen to prove what I have just said:

"Mary has two sons, the one a God-man, the other, mere man. She is Mother of the first corporally and of the second spiritually" (St. Bonaventure and Origen).

"This is the will of God who willed that we should have all things through Mary. If then, we possess any hope or grace or gift of salvation, let us acknowledge that it comes to us through her" (St. Bernard).

"All the gifts, graces, virtues of the Holy Spirit are distributed by the hands of Mary, to whom she wills, when she wills, as she wills, and in the measure she wills" (St. Bernardine).

"As you were not worthy that anything divine should be given to you, all graces were given to Mary so that you might receive through her all graces you would not otherwise receive" (St. Bernard).

142. St. Bernard tells us that God, seeing that we are unworthy to receive his graces directly from him, gives them to Mary so that we might receive from her all that he decides to give us. His glory is achieved when he receives through Mary the gratitude, respect and love we owe him in return for his gifts to us. It is only right then that we should imitate his conduct, "in order", as St. Bernard again says, "that grace might return to its author by the same channel through which it came to us."

This is what we do by this devotion. We offer and consecrate all we are and all we possess to the Blessed Virgin in order that our Lord may receive through her as intermediary the glory and gratitude that we owe to him. We deem ourselves unworthy and unfit to approach his infinite majesty on our own, and so we avail ourselves of Mary's intercession.

143. Moreover, this devotion is an expression of great humility, a virtue which God loves above all others. A person who exalts himself debases God, and a person who humbles himself exalts God. "God opposes the proud, but gives his graces to the humble."* If you humble yourself, convinced that you are unworthy to appear before him, or even to approach him, he condescends to come down to you. He is pleased to be with you and exalts you in spite of yourself. But, on the other hand, if you venture to go towards God boldly without a mediator, he vanishes and is nowhere to be found. How dearly he loves the humble of heart! It is to such humility that this devotion leads us, for it teaches us never to go alone directly to our Lord, however gentle and merciful though he may be, but always to use Mary's power of intercession, whether we want to enter his presence, speak to him, be near him, offer him something, seek union with him or consecrate ourselves to him.

3. It obtains many blessings from our Lady.

144. The Blessed Virgin, mother of gentleness and mercy, never allows herself to be surpassed in love and generosity. When she sees someone giving himself entirely to her in order to honour and serve her, and depriving himself of what he prizes most in order to adorn her, she gives herself completely in a wondrous manner to him. She engulfs him in the ocean of her graces, adorns him with her merits, supports him with her power, enlightens him with her light, and fills him with her love.

* Jas. 4:6.

She shares her virtues with him — her humility, faith, purity, etc. She makes up for his failings and becomes his representative with Jesus. Just as one who is consecrated belongs entirely to Mary, so Mary belongs entirely to him. We can truthfully say of this perfect servant and child of Mary what St. John in his gospel says of himself, "He took her for his own."

145. This produces in his soul, if he is persevering, a great distrust, contempt, and hatred of self, and a great confidence in Mary with complete self-abandonment to her. He no longer relies on his own dispositions, intentions, merits, virtues and good works, since he has sacrificed them completely to Jesus through his loving Mother. He has now only one treasury, where all his wealth is stored. That treasury is not within himself: it is Mary. That is why he can now go to our Lord without any servile or scrupulous fear and pray to him with great confidence. He can share the sentiments of the devout and learned Abbot Rupert, who, referring to the victory which Jacob won over an angel,* addressed our Lady in these words, "O Mary, my Queen, Immaculate Mother of the God-man, Jesus Christ, I desire to wrestle with this man, the Divine Word, armed with your merits and not my own."

How much stronger and more powerful are we in approaching our Lord when we are armed with the merits and prayers of the worthy Mother of God, who, as St. Augustine says, has conquered the Almighty by her love!

146. Since by this devotion we give to our Lord, through the hands of his holy Mother, all our good works, she purifies them, making them beautiful and acceptable to her Son.

1) She purifies them of every taint of self-love and of that unconscious attachment to creatures

* Gen. 32:25.

which slips unnoticed into our best actions. Her hands have never been known to be idle or uncreative. They purify everything they touch. As soon as the Blessed Virgin receives our good works, she removes any blemish or imperfection she may find in them.

147. 2) She enriches our good works by adorning them with her own merits and virtues. It is as if a poor peasant, wishing to win the friendship and favour of the king, were to go to the queen and give her an apple — his only possession — for her to offer it to the king. The queen, accepting the peasant's humble gift, puts it on a beautiful golden dish and presents it to the king on behalf of the peasant. The apple in itself would not be a gift worthy of a king, but presented by the queen in person on a dish of gold, it becomes fit for any king.

148. 3) Mary presents our good works to Jesus. She does not keep anything we offer for herself, as if she were our last end, but unfailingly gives everything to Jesus. So by the very fact we give anything to her, we are giving it to Jesus. Whenever we praise and glorify her, she immediately praises and glorifies Jesus. When anyone praises and blesses her, she sings today as she did on the day Elizabeth praised her, *"My soul glorifies the Lord."*

149. At Mary's request, Jesus accepts the gift of our good works, no matter how poor and insignificant they may be for one who is the King of kings, the Holiest of the holy. When we present anything to Jesus by ourselves, relying on our own dispositions and efforts, he examines our gift and often rejects it because it is stained with self-love, imbued with selfish motives.

But when we present something to him by the pure, virginal hands of his beloved Mother, we take him by his weak side, in a manner of speaking. He does not consider so much the present itself as the person who offers it. Thus Mary, who is never slighted by her Son but is always well received, prevails upon him to accept with pleasure everything she offers him, regardless of its value. This is what St. Bernard strongly recommended to all those he was guiding along the pathway to perfection. *"When you want to offer something to God, to be welcomed by him be sure to offer it through the worthy Mother of God, if you do not wish to see it rejected."*

150. Does not human nature itself, as we have seen, suggest this mode of procedure to the less important people of this world with regard to the great? Why should grace not inspire us to do likewise with regard to God? He is infinitely exalted above us. We are less than atoms in his sight. But we have an advocate so powerful that she is never refused anything. She is so resourceful that she knows every secret way to win the heart of God. She is so good and kind that she never passes over anyone no matter how lowly and sinful.

Further on, I shall relate the story of Jacob and Rebecca which exemplifies the truths I have been setting before you.

4. It is an excellent means of giving glory to God

151. This devotion, when faithfully undertaken, is a perfect means of ensuring that the value of all our good works is being used for the greater glory of God. Scarcely anyone works for that noble end, in spite of the obligation to do so, either because men do not know where God's greatest glory is to be found or because they do not desire it. Now Mary, to whom we surrender the value and merit of our good actions, knows perfectly well where God's greatest glory lies and she works only to promote that glory.

The devout servant of our Lady, having entirely consecrated himself to her as we have described above, can boldly claim that the value of all his actions, words, and thoughts is used for the greatest glory of God, unless he has explicitly retracted his offering. For one who loves God with a pure and unselfish love and prizes God's glory and interests far above his own, could anything be more consoling?

5. It leads to union with our Lord

152. This devotion is a smooth, short, perfect and sure way of attaining union with our Lord, in which Christian perfection consists.

1) *This devotion is a smooth way.* It is the path which Jesus Christ opened up in coming to us and in which there is no obstruction to prevent our reaching him. It is quite true that we can attain to divine union by other roads, but these involve many more crosses and exceptional setbacks and many difficulties that we cannot easily overcome. We would have to pass through spiritual darkness, engage in struggles for which we are not prepared, endure bitter agonies, scale precipitous mountains, tread upon painful thorns, and cross frightful deserts. But when we take the path of Mary, we walk smoothly and calmly.

It is true that on our way we have hard battles to fight and serious obstacles to overcome, but Mary, our Mother and Queen, stays close to her faithful servants. She is always at hand to brighten their darkness, clear away their doubts, strengthen them in their fears, sustain them in their combats and trials. Truly, in comparison with other ways, this virgin road to Jesus is a path of roses and sweet delights. There have been some saints, not very many, such as St. Ephrem, St. John Damascene, St. Bernard, St. Bernardine, St. Bonaventure and St. Francis de Sales, who have taken this smooth path to Jesus Christ, because the Holy Spirit, the faithful Spouse of Mary, made it known to them by a special grace. The other saints, who are the greater number, while having a devotion to Mary, either did not enter or did not go far along this path. That is why they had to undergo harder and more dangerous trials.

153. Why is it then, a servant of Mary might ask, that devoted servants of this good Mother are called upon to suffer much more than those who serve her less generously? They are opposed, persecuted, slandered, and treated with intolerance. They may also have to walk in interior darkness and through spiritual deserts without being given from heaven a single drop of the dew of consolation. If this devotion to the Blessed Virgin makes the path to Jesus smoother, how can we explain why Mary's loyal servants are so ill-treated?

154. I reply that it is quite true that the most faithful servants of the Blessed Virgin, being her greatest favourites, receive from her the best graces and favours from heaven, which are crosses. But I maintain too that these servants of Mary bear their crosses with greater ease and gain more merit and glory. What could check another's progress a thousand times over, or possibly bring about his downfall, does not balk them at all, but even helps them on their way. For this good Mother, filled with the grace and unction of the Holy Spirit, dips all the crosses she prepares for them in the honey of her maternal sweetness and the unction of pure love. They then readily swallow them as they would sugared almonds, though the crosses may be very bitter. I believe that anyone who wishes to be devout and live piously in Jesus will suffer persecution* and will have a daily

* 2 Tim.3:12.

cross to carry. But he will never manage to carry a heavy cross, or carry it joyfully and perseveringly, without a trusting devotion to our Lady, who is the very sweetness of the cross. It is obvious that a person could not keep on eating without great effort unripe fruit which has not been sweetened.

155. 2) *This devotion is a short way* to discover Jesus, either because it is a road we do not wander from, or because, as we have just said, we walk along this road with greater ease and joy, and consequently with greater speed. We advance more in a brief period of submission to Mary and dependence on her than in whole years of self-will and self-reliance. A man who is obedient and submissive to Mary will sing of glorious victories over his enemies. It is true, his enemies will try to impede his progress, force him to retreat or try to make him fall. But with Mary's help, support and guidance, he will go forward towards our Lord. Without falling, retreating and even without being delayed, he will advance with giant strides towards Jesus along the same road which, as is written, Jesus took to come to us with giant strides* and in a short time.*

156. Why do you think our Lord spent only a few years here on earth and nearly all of them in submission and obedience to his Mother? The reason is that "attaining perfection in a short time, he lived a long time",† even longer than Adam, whose losses he had come to make good. Yet Adam lived more than nine hundred years!

Jesus lived a long time, because he lived in complete submission to his Mother and in union with her, which obedience to God his Father required. The Holy Spirit tells us that the man who honours his mother

* Ps. 18:6.   † Wis. 4:13.

is like a man who stores up a treasure.* In other words, the man who honours Mary, his Mother, to the extent of subjecting himself to her and obeying her in all things will soon become very rich, because he is amassing riches every day through Mary who has become his secret philosopher's stone.

There is another quotation from Holy Scripture, *"My old age will be found in the mercy of the bosom."*† According to the mystical interpretation of these words it is in the bosom of Mary that people who are young grow mature in enlightenment, in holiness, in experience and in wisdom, and in a short time reach the fulness of the age of Christ. For it was Mary's womb which encompassed and produced a perfect man. That same womb held the one whom the whole universe can neither encompass nor contain.

157. 3) *This devotion is a perfect way* to reach our Lord and be united to him, for Mary is the most perfect and the most holy of all creatures, and Jesus, who came to us in a perfect manner, chose no other road for his great and wonderful journey. The Most High, the Incomprehensible One, the Inaccessible One, He who is, deigned to come down to us poor earthly creatures who are nothing at all. How was this done?

The Most High God came down to us in a perfect way through the humble Virgin Mary, without losing anything of his divinity or holiness. It is likewise through Mary that we poor creatures must ascend to almighty God in a perfect manner without having anything to fear.

God, the Incomprehensible, allowed himself to be perfectly comprehended and contained by the humble Virgin Mary without losing anything of his

* Ecclus. 3:5.

† A former interpretation of Ps.91:11 based on a mistranslation.

majesty. So it is also through Mary that we must draw near to God and unite ourselves to him perfectly, intimately, and without fear of being rejected.

Lastly, He who is deigned to come down to us who are not and turned our nothingness into God, or He who is. He did this perfectly by giving and submitting himself entirely to the young Virgin Mary without ceasing to be in time He who is from all eternity. Likewise it is through Mary that we, who are nothing, may become like God by grace and glory. We accomplish this by giving ourselves to her so perfectly and so completely as to remain nothing, as far as self is concerned, and to be everything in her, without any fear of illusion.

158. Show me a new road to our Lord, pave it with all the merits of the saints, adorn it with their heroic virtues, illuminate and enhance it with the splendour and beauty of the angels, have all the angels and saints there to guide and protect those who wish to follow it. Give me such a road and truly, I boldly say, — and I am telling the truth — that instead of this road, perfect though it be, I would still choose the immaculate way of Mary. It is a way, a road without stain or spot, without original sin or actual sin, without shadow or darkness. When our loving Jesus comes in glory once again to reign upon earth — as he certainly will — he will choose no other way than the Blessed Virgin, by whom he came so surely and so perfectly the first time. The difference between his first and his second coming is that the first was secret and hidden, but the second will be glorious and resplendent. Both are perfect because both are through Mary. Alas, this is a mystery which we cannot understand. *"Here let every tongue be silent."*

159. 4) *This devotion to our Lady is a sure way* to go to Jesus and to acquire holiness through union with him.

a) The devotion which I teach is not new. Its history goes back so far that the time of its origin cannot be ascertained with any precision, as Fr. Boudon, who died a short time ago in the odour of sanctity, states in a book which he wrote on this devotion.* It is however certain that for more than seven hundred years we find traces of it in the Church.

St. Odilo, abbot of Cluny, who lived about the year 1040, was one of the first to practise it publicly in France as is told in his life.

Cardinal Peter Damian relates that in the year 1076 his brother, Blessed Marino, made himself the slave of the Blessed Virgin in the presence of his spiritual director in a most edifying manner. He placed a rope around his neck, scourged himself and placed on the altar a sum of money as a token of his devotion and consecration to our Lady. He remained so faithful to this consecration all his life that he merited to be visited and consoled on his deathbed by his dear Queen and hear from her lips the promise of paradise in reward for his service.

Caesarius Bollandus mentions a famous knight, Vautier de Birbak, a close relative of the Dukes of Louvain, who about the year 1300 consecrated himself to the Blessed Virgin.

This devotion was also practised privately by many people up to the seventeenth century, when it became publicly known.

160. Father Simon de Rojas of the order of the Holy Trinity for the Redemption of Captives, court preacher

---

* Henri-Marie Boudon (1624-1702), Archdeacon of Evreux, author of *God alone or the Holy Slavery of the Admirable Mother of God.* Boudon says in this book that English Catholics were noted for the practice of this devotion.

to Philip III, made this devotion popular throughout Spain and Germany. Through the intervention of Philip III, he obtained from Gregory XV valuable indulgences for those who practised it.

Father de Los Rios of the order of St. Augustine, together with his intimate friend, Father de Rojas, worked hard, propagating it throughout Spain and Germany by preaching and writing. He composed a large volume entitled *Hierarchia Mariana,* where he treats of the antiquity, the excellence and the soundness of this devotion, with as much devotion as learning.

The Theatine Fathers in the seventeenth century established this devotion in Italy, Sicily and Savoy.

161. Father Stanislaus Phalacius of the Society of Jesus spread this devotion widely in Poland.

Father de Los Rios in the book quoted above mentions the names of princes and princesses, bishops and cardinals of different countries who embraced this devotion.

Father Cornelius a Lapide, noted both for holiness and profound learning, was commissioned by several bishops and theologians to examine it. The praise he gave it after mature examination, is a worthy tribute to his own holiness. Many other eminent men followed his example.

The Jesuit Fathers, ever zealous in the service of our Blessed Lady, presented on behalf of the sodalities of Cologne to Duke Ferdinand of Bavaria, the then archbishop of Cologne, a little treatise on the devotion, and he gave it his approval and granted permission to have it printed. He exhorted all priests and religious of his diocese to do their utmost to spread this solid devotion.

162. Cardinal de Bérulle, whose memory is venerated throughout France, was outstandingly zealous in furthering the devotion in France, despite the calumnies and persecution he suffered at the hands of critics and evil men. They accused him of introducing novelty and superstition. They composed and published a libellous tract against him and they — or rather the devil in them — used a thousand stratagems to prevent him from spreading the devotion in France. But this eminent and saintly man responded to their calumnies with calm patience. He wrote a little book in reply to their libel and forcefully refuted the objections contained in it. He pointed out that this devotion is founded on the example given by Jesus Christ, on the obligations we have towards him and on the promises we made in holy baptism. It was mainly this last reason which silenced his enemies. He made clear to them that this consecration to the Blessed Virgin, and through her to Jesus, is nothing less than a perfect renewal of the promises and vows of baptism. He said many beautiful things concerning this devotion which can be read in his works.

163 In Fr. Boudon's book we read of the different popes who gave their approval to this devotion, the theologians who examined it, the hostility it encountered and overcame, the thousands who made it their own without censure from any pope. Indeed it could not be condemned without overthrowing the foundations of Christianity.

It is obvious then that this devotion is not new. If it is not commonly practised, the reason is that it is too sublime to be appreciated and undertaken by everyone.

164. *b)* This devotion is a safe means of going to Jesus Christ, because it is Mary's role to lead us safely to her Son; just as it is the role of our Lord to lead us to the eternal Father. Those who are spiritually-minded should not fall into the error of thinking that Mary hinders our union with God. How could this possibly happen? How could Mary, who found grace with God for everyone in general and each one in particular, prevent a soul from obtaining the supreme grace of union with him?

It is quite true that the example of other people, no matter how holy, can sometimes impair union with God, but not so our Blessed Lady, as I have said and shall never weary of repeating. One reason why so few souls come to the fulness of the age of Jesus is that Mary who is still as much as ever his Mother and the fruitful spouse of the Holy Spirit is not formed well enough in their hearts. If we desire a ripe and perfectly formed fruit, we must possess the tree that bears it. If we desire the fruit of life, Jesus Christ, we must possess the tree of life which is Mary. If we desire to have the Holy Spirit working within us, we must possess his faithful and inseparable spouse, Mary, whom as I have said elsewhere, he can make fruitful.

165. Rest assured that the more you turn to Mary in your prayers, meditations, actions and sufferings, seeing her if not perhaps clearly and distinctly, at least in a general and indistinct way, the more surely will you discover Jesus. For he is always greater, more powerful, more active and more mysterious when acting through Mary than he is in any other creature in the universe, or even in heaven. Thus Mary, so divinely-favoured and so lost in God, is far from being an obstacle to good people who are striving for union with him. There has never been and there never will be a creature so ready to help us in achieving that union more effectively, for she will dispense to us all the graces to attain that end. As a saint once remarked, *"Only Mary knows how to fill our minds with the thought of God"*. Moreover

Mary will safeguard us against the deception and cunning of the evil one.

166. Where Mary is present, the evil one is absent. One of the unmistakable signs that a person is led by the spirit of God is the devotion he has to Mary, and his habit of thinking and speaking of her. This is the opinion of a saint, who goes on to say that just as breathing is a proof that the body is not dead, so the habitual thought of Mary and loving converse with her is a proof that the soul is not spiritually dead in sin.

167. Since Mary alone has crushed all heresies, as we are told by the Church under the guidance of the Holy Spirit, (Office of B.V.M.), a devoted servant of hers will never fall into formal heresy or error, though critics may contest this. He may very well err materially, mistaking lies for truth or an evil spirit for a good one, but he will be less likely to do this than others. Sooner or later he will discover his error and will not go on stubbornly believing and maintaining what he mistakenly thought was the truth.

168. Whoever then wishes to advance along the road to holiness and be sure of encountering the true Christ, without fear of the illusions which afflict many devout people, should take up "with valiant heart and willing spirit"* this devotion to Mary which perhaps he had not heard about. Even if it is new to him, let him enter upon this excellent way which I am now revealing to him. "I will show you a more excellent way."†

It was opened up by Jesus Christ, the Incarnate Wisdom. He is our one and only Head, and we, his members, cannot go wrong in following him. It is a *smooth* way made easy by the fulness of grace, the unction of the Holy Spirit. In our progress along this road, we do not weaken or turn back. It is a *quick* way

* 2 Macc. 1:3. † 1 Cor. 12:31.

and leads us to Jesus in a short time. It is a *perfect* way without mud or dust or any vileness of sin. Finally, it is a reliable way, for it is *direct* and *sure,* having no turnings to right or left but leading us straight to Jesus and to life eternal.

Let us then take this road and travel along it night and day until we arrive at the fulness of the age of Jesus Christ.

6. It gives liberty of spirit

169. *This devotion gives great liberty of spirit* — the freedom of the children of God — to those who faithfully practise it. Through this devotion we make ourselves slaves of Jesus by consecrating ourselves entirely to him. To reward us for this enslavement of love, our Lord frees us from every scruple and servile fear which might restrict, imprison or confuse us; he opens our hearts and fills them with holy confidence in God, helping us to regard God as our Father; he inspires us with a generous and filial love.

170. Without stopping to prove this truth, I shall simply relate an incident which I read in the life of Mother Agnes of Jesus, a Dominican nun of the convent of Langeac in Auvergne, who died there in the odour of sanctity in 1634.

When she was only seven years old and was suffering great spiritual anguish, she heard a voice telling her that if she wished to be delivered from her anguish and protected against all her enemies, she should make herself the slave of our Lord and his Blessed Mother as soon as possible. No sooner had she returned home than she gave herself completely to Jesus and Mary as their slave, although she had never known anything about this devotion before. She found an iron chain, put it round her waist and wore it till the day she died. After this, all her sufferings and scruples disappeared and she found great peace of soul.

This led her to teach this devotion to many others who made rapid progress in it — among them, Father Olier, the founder of the Seminary of St. Sulpice, and several other priests and students from the same seminary. One day the Blessed Virgin appeared to Mother Agnes and put a gold chain around her neck to show her how happy she was that Mother Agnes had become the slave of both her and her Son. And St. Cecilia, who accompanied our Lady, said to her, *"Happy are the faithful slaves of the Queen of heaven, for they will enjoy true freedom. "Tibi servire libertas.*

7.   It is of great benefit to our neighbour

171.   By this devotion we show love for our neighbour in an outstanding way, since we give him through Mary's hands all that we prize most highly — that is, the satisfactory and prayer value of all our good works, down to the least good thought and the least little suffering. We give our consent that all we have already acquired or will acquire until death should be used in accordance with our Lady's will for the conversion of sinners or the deliverance of souls from purgatory.

Is this not perfect love of our neighbour? Is this not being a true disciple of our Lord, one who should always be recognised by his love? Is this not the way to convert sinners without any danger of vainglory, and deliver souls from purgatory by doing hardly anything more than what we are obliged to do by our state of life?

172.   To appreciate the excellence of this motive we must understand what a wonderful thing it is to convert a sinner or to deliver a soul from purgatory. It is an infinite good, greater than the creation of heaven and earth, since it gives a soul the possession of God. If by this devotion we secured the release of only one soul from purgatory or converted only one sinner in our whole lifetime, would that not be enough to induce any person who really loves his neighbour to practise this devotion?

It must be noted that our good works, passing through Mary's hands, are progressively purified. Consequently, their merit and their satisfactory and prayer value is also increased. That is why they become much more effective in relieving the souls in purgatory and in converting sinners than if they did not pass through the virginal and liberal hands of Mary. Stripped of self-will and clothed with disinterested love, the little that we give to the Blessed Virgin is truly powerful enough to appease the anger of God and draw down his mercy. It may well be that at the hour of death a person who has been faithful to this devotion will find that he has freed many souls from purgatory and converted many sinners, even though he performed only the ordinary actions of his state of life. Great will be his joy at the judgement. Great will be his glory throughout eternity.

8. It is a wonderful means of perseverance

173.   Finally, what draws us in a sense more compellingly to take up this devotion to the most Blessed Virgin is the fact that it is a wonderful means of persevering in the practice of virtue and of remaining steadfast.

Why is it that most conversions of sinners are not lasting? Why do they relapse so easily into sin? Why is it that most of the faithful, instead of making progress in one virtue after another and so acquiring new graces, often lose the little grace and virtue they have? This misfortune arises, as I have shown, from the fact that man, so prone to evil, so weak and changeable, trusts himself too much, relies on his own strength, and wrongly presumes he is able to safeguard his precious graces, virtues and merits.

By this devotion we entrust all we possess to Mary, the faithful Virgin. We choose her as the guardian of all our possessions in the natural and supernatural sphere. We trust her because she is faithful, we rely on her strength, we count on her mercy and charity to preserve and increase our virtues and merits in spite of the efforts of the devil, the world, and the flesh to rob us of them. We say to her as a good child would say to its mother or a faithful servant to the mistress of the house, "My dear Mother and Mistress, I realise that up to now I have received from God through your intercession more graces than I deserve. But bitter experience has taught me that I carry these riches in a very fragile vessel and that I am too weak and sinful to guard them by myself. Please accept in trust everything I possess, and in your faithfulness and power keep it for me. If you watch over me, I shall lose nothing. If you support me, I shall not fall. If you protect me, I shall be safe from my enemies."

174. This is exactly what St. Bernard clearly pointed out to encourage us to take up this devotion, *"When Mary supports you, you will not fall. With her as your protector, you will have nothing to fear. With her as your guide you will not grow weary. When you win her favour, you will reach the port of heaven."* St. Bonaventure seems to say the same thing in even more explicit terms, *"The Blessed Virgin,"* he says, *not only preserves the fulness enjoyed by the saints, but she* *maintains the saints in their fulness so that it does not diminish. She prevents their virtues from fading away, their merits from being wasted and their graces from being lost. She prevents the devils from doing them harm and she so influences them that her divine Son has no need to punish them when they sin."*

175. Mary is the Virgin most faithful who by her fidelity to God makes good the losses caused by Eve's unfaithfulness. She obtains fidelity to God and final perseverance for those who commit themselves to her. For this reason St. John Damascene compared her to a firm anchor which holds them fast and saves them from shipwreck in the raging seas of the world where so many people perish through lack of such a firm anchor. *"We fasten souls,"* he said, *"to Mary, our hope, as to a firm anchor."* It was to Mary that the saints who attained salvation most firmly anchored themselves as did others who wanted to ensure their perseverance in their holiness.

Blessed, indeed, are those Christians who bind themselves faithfully and completely to her as to a secure anchor! The violent storms of the world will not make them founder or carry away their heavenly riches. Blessed are those who enter into her as into another Noah's ark! The flood waters of sin which engulf so many will not harm them because, as the Church makes Mary say in the words of divine Wisdom, *"Those who work with my help — for their salvation — shall not sin."* Blessed are the unfaithful children of unhappy Eve who commit themselves to Mary, the ever-faithful Virgin and Mother who never wavers in her fidelity and never goes back on her trust. She always loves those who love her, not only with deep affection, but with a love that is active and generous. By an abundant outpouring of grace she keeps them from relaxing their effort in the practice of virtue or falling by the wayside through loss of divine grace.

176. Moved by pure love, this good Mother always accepts whatever is given her in trust, and, once she accepts something, she binds herself in justice by a contract of trusteeship to keep it safe. Is not someone to whom I entrust the sum of a thousand francs obliged to keep it safe for me so that if it were lost through his negligence he would be responsible for it in strict justice? But nothing we entrust to the faithful Virgin will ever be lost through her negligence. Heaven and earth would pass away sooner than Mary would neglect or betray those who trusted in her.

177. Poor children of Mary, you are extremely weak and changeable. Your human nature is deeply impaired. It is sadly true that you have been fashioned from the same corrupted nature as the other children of Adam and Eve. But do not let that discourage you. Rejoice and be glad! Here is a secret which I am revealing to you, a secret unknown to most Christians, even the most devout.

Do not leave your gold and silver in your own safes which have already been broken into and rifled many times by the evil one. They are too small, too flimsy and too old to contain such great and priceless possessions. Do not put pure and clear water from the spring into vessels fouled and infected by sin. Even if sin is no longer there, its odour persists and the water would be contaminated. You do not put choice wine into old casks that have contained sour wine. You would spoil the good wine and run the risk of losing it.

178. Chosen souls, although you may already understand me, I shall express myself still more clearly. Do not commit the gold of your charity, the silver of your purity to a threadbare sack or a battered old chest, or the waters of heavenly grace or the wines of your merits and virtues to a tainted and fetid cask, such as you are. Otherwise you will be robbed by thieving devils who are on the look-out day and night waiting for a favourable opportunity to plunder. If you do so, all those pure gifts from God will be spoiled by the unwholesome presence of self-love, inordinate self-reliance and self-will.

Pour into the bosom and heart of Mary all your precious possessions, all your graces and virtues. She is a spiritual vessel, a vessel of honour, a singular vessel of devotion. Ever since God personally hid himself with all his perfections in this vessel, it has become completely spiritual, and the spiritual abode of all spiritual souls. It has become honourable and has been the throne of honour for the greatest saints in heaven. It has become outstanding in devotion and the home of those renowned for gentleness, grace and virtue. Moreover, it has become as rich as a house of gold, as strong as a tower of David and as pure as a tower of ivory.

179. Blessed is the man who has given everything to Mary, who at all times and in all things trusts in her, and loses himself in her. He belongs to Mary and Mary belongs to him. With David he can boldly say, "She was created for me," or with the beloved disciple, "I have taken her for my own", or with our Lord himself, "All that is mine is yours and all that is yours is mine".

180. If any critic reading this should imagine that I am exaggerating or speaking from an excess of devotion, he has not, alas, understood what I have said. Either he is a carnal man who has no taste for the spiritual; or he is a worldly man who has cut himself off from the Holy Spirit; or he is a proud and critical man who ridicules and condemns anything he does not understand But those who are born not of blood, nor of flesh, nor

of the will of man, but of God and of Mary, understand and appreciate what I have to say. It is for them that I am writing.

181. Nevertheless after this digression, I say to both the critics and the devout that the Blessed Virgin, the most reliable and generous of all God's creatures, never lets herself by surpassed by anyone in love and generosity. For the little that is given to her, she gives generously of what she has received from God. Consequently, if a person gives himself to her without reserve, she gives herself also without reserve to that person provided his confidence in her is not presumptuous and he does his best to practise virtue and curb his passions.

182. So the faithful servants of the Blessed Virgin may confidently say with St. John Damascene, *"If I confide in you, Mother of God, I shall be saved. Under your protection I shall fear nothing. With your help I shall rout all my enemies. For devotion to you is a weapon of salvation which God gives to those he wishes to save"* (Joan. Damas. ser. de Annuntiat).

CHAPTER FIVE

BIBLICAL FIGURE OF THIS PERFECT DEVOTION: REBECCA AND JACOB

183.   The Holy Spirit gives us in Sacred Scripture a striking allegorical figure of all the truths I have been explaining concerning the Blessed Virgin and her children and servants. It is the story of Jacob who received the blessing of his father Isaac through the care and ingenuity of his mother Rebecca.

Here is the story as the Holy Spirit tells it. I shall expound it further later on.

The Story of Jacob

184.   Several years after Esau had sold his birthright to Jacob, Rebecca, their mother, who loved Jacob tenderly, secured this blessing for him by a holy stratagem full of mystery for us.

Isaac, realizing that he was getting old, wished to bless his children before he died. He summoned Esau, who was his favourite son, and told him to go out hunting and bring him something to eat, in order that he might then give him his blessing. Rebecca immediately told Jacob what was happening and sent him to fetch two small goats from the flock. When Jacob gave them to his mother, she cooked them in the way Isaac liked them. Then she dressed Jacob in Esau's clothes which she had in her keeping, and covered his hands and neck with the goat-skin. The father, who was blind, although hearing the voice of Jacob, would think that it was Esau when he touched the skin on his hands.

Isaac was of course surprised at the voice which he thought was Jacob's and told him to come closer.

Isaac felt the hair on the skin covering Jacob's hands and said that the voice was indeed like Jacob's but the hands were Esau's. After he had eaten, Isaac kissed Jacob and smelt the fragrance of his scented clothes. He blessed him and called down on him the dew of heaven and the fruitfulness of earth. He made him master of all his brothers and concluded his blessing with these words, "Cursed be those who curse you and blessed be those who bless you."

Isaac had scarcely finished speaking when Esau came in, bringing what he had caught while out hunting. He wanted his father to bless him after he had eaten. The holy patriarch was shocked when he realized what had happened. But far from retracting what he had done, he confirmed it because he clearly saw the finger of God in it all. Then as Holy Scripture relates, Esau began to protest loudly against the treachery of his brother. He then asked his father if he had only one blessing to give. In so doing, as the early Fathers point out, Esau was the symbol of those who are too ready to imagine that there is an alliance between God and the world, because they themselves are eager to enjoy at one and the same time, the blessings of heaven and the blessings of the earth. Isaac was touched by Esau's cries and finally blessed him but only with a blessing of the earth, and he subjected him to his brother. Because of this, Esau conceived such a venomous hatred for Jacob that he could hardly wait for his father's death to kill him. And Jacob would not have escaped death if his dear mother Rebecca had not saved him by her ingenuity and her good advice.

Interpretation of the story

185. Before explaining this beautiful story, let me

remind you that, according to the early Fathers and the interpreters of Holy Scripture, Jacob is the type of our Lord and of souls who are saved, and Esau is the type of souls who are condemned. We have only to examine the actions and conduct of both in order to judge each one.

1) Esau, the elder brother, was strong and robust, clever, and skilful with the bow and very successful at hunting.

2) He seldom stayed at home and, relying only on his own strength and skill, worked out of doors.

3) He never went out of his way to please his mother Rebecca, and did little or nothing for her.

4) He was such a glutton and so fond of eating that he sold his birthright for a dish of lentils.

5) Like Cain, he was extremely jealous of his brother and persecuted him relentlessly.

186. This is the usual conduct of sinners:

1) They rely upon their own strength and skill in temporal affairs. They are very energetic, clever and well-informed about things of this world but very dull and ignorant about things of heaven.

187. *2)* And so they are never or very seldom at home, in their own house, that is, in their own interior, the inner, essential abode that God has given to every man to dwell in, after his own example, for God always abides within himself. Sinners have no liking for solitude or the spiritual life or interior devotion. They consider those who live an interior life, secluded from the world, and who work more interiorly than exteriorly, as narrow-minded, bigoted and uncivilized.

188. *3)* Sinners care little or nothing about devotion to Mary the Mother of the elect. It is true that they do not really hate her. Indeed they even speak well of her sometimes. They say they love her and they practise some devotion in her honour. Nevertheless they cannot bear to see anyone love her tenderly, for they do not have for her any of the affection of Jacob; they find fault with the honour which her good children and servants faithfully pay her to win her affection. They think this kind of devotion is not necessary for salvation, and as long as they do not go as far as hating her or openly ridiculing devotion to her they believe they have done all they need to win her good graces. Because they recite or mumble a few prayers to her without any affection and without even thinking of amending their lives, they consider they are our Lady's servants.

189. *4)* Sinners sell their birthright, that is, the joys of paradise, for a dish of lentils, that is, the pleasures of this world. They laugh, they drink, they eat, they have a good time, they gamble, they dance and so forth, without taking any more trouble than Esau to make themselves worthy of their heavenly Father's blessing. Briefly, they think only of this world, love only the world, speak and act only for the world and its pleasures. For a passing moment of pleasure, for a fleeting wisp of honour, for a piece of hard earth, yellow or white* they barter away their baptismal grace, their robe of innocence and their heavenly inheritance.

190. *5)* Finally, sinners continually hate and persecute the elect, openly or secretly. The elect are a burden to them. They despise them, criticize them, ridicule them, insult them, rob them, deceive them, impoverish them, hunt them down and trample them into the dust; while they themselves are making fortunes, enjoying themselves, getting good positions for themselves, enriching themselves, rising to power and living in comfort.

---

* Favourite expression of St. Louis Marie for gold and silver.

191. *1)* Jacob, the younger son, was of a frail constitution, gentle and peaceable, and usually stayed at home to please his mother, whom he loved so much. If he did go out it was not through any personal desire of his, nor from any confidence in his own ability, but simply out of obedience to his mother.

192. *2)* He loved and honoured his mother. That is why he remained at home close to her. He was never happier than when he was in her presence. He avoided everything that might displease her, and did everything he thought would please her. This made Rebecca love him all the more.

193. *3)* He was submissive to his mother in all things. He obeyed her entirely in everything, promptly without delay and lovingly without complaint. At the least indication of her will, young Jacob hastened to comply with it. He accepted whatever she told him without questioning. For instance, when she told him to get two small goats and bring them to her so that she might prepare something for his father Isaac to eat, Jacob did not reply that one would be enough for one man, but without arguing he did exactly what she told him to do.

194. *4)* He had the utmost confidence in his mother. He did not rely on his own ability; he relied solely on his mother's care and protection. He went to her in all his needs and consulted her in all his doubts. For instance, when he asked her if his father, instead of blessing him, would curse him, he believed her and trusted her when she said she would take the curse upon herself.

195. *5)* Finally, he adopted, as much as he could, the virtues he saw in his mother. It seems that one of the reasons why he spent so much time at home was to imitate his dear mother, who was so virtuous, and to keep away from evil companions, who might lead him into sin. In this way, he made himself worthy to receive the double blessing of his beloved father.

196. It is in a similar manner that God's chosen ones usually act.

1) They stay at home with their mother — that is, they have an esteem for quietness, love the interior life and are assiduous in prayer. They always remain in the company of the Blessed Virgin, their Mother and Model, whose glory is wholly interior and who during her whole life dearly loved seclusion and prayer. It is true, at times they do venture out into the world, but only to fulfil the duties of their state of life, in obedience to the will of God and the will of their Mother.

No matter how great their accomplishments may appear to others, they attach far more importance to what they do within themselves in their interior life, in the company of the Blessed Virgin. For there they work at the great task of perfection, compared to which all other work is mere child's play. At times their brothers and sisters are working outside with great energy, skill and success, and win the praise and approbation of the world. But they know by the light of the Holy Spirit, that there is far more good, more glory and more joy in remaining hidden and recollected with our Lord, in complete and perfect submission to Mary, than there is in performing by themselves marvellous works of nature and grace in the world like so many Esaus and sinners. Glory for God and riches for men are in her house*.

Lord Jesus, how lovely is your dwelling place! The sparrow has found a home to dwell in, and the turtle-dove a nest for her little ones!† How happy is the man who dwells in the house of Mary, where you

* Ps.111:3.   † Ps. 83:4.

were the first to dwell! Here in this home of the elect, he draws from you alone the help he needs to climb the stairway of virtue he has built in his heart to the highest possible point of perfection while in this vale of tears.

197. *2)* The elect have a great love for our Lady and honour her truly as their Mother and Queen. They love her not merely in word but in deed. They honour her not just outwardly, but from the depths of their heart. Like Jacob, they avoid the least thing that might displease her, and eagerly do whatever they think might win her favour. As Jacob brought Rebecca two young goats, they bring Mary their body and their soul, with all their faculties,

a) that she may accept them as her own;

b) that she may make them die to sin and self by divesting them of self-love, in order to please Jesus her Son, who wishes to have as friends and disciples only those who are dead to sin and self,

c) that she may clothe them according to their heavenly Father's taste and for his greater glory, which she knows better than any other creature,

d) that through her care and intercession, this body and soul of theirs, thoroughly cleansed from every stain, thoroughly dead to self, thoroughly stripped and well-prepared, may be pleasing to the heavenly Father and deserving of his blessing.

Is this not what those chosen souls do who, to prove to Jesus and Mary how effective and courageous is their love, live and esteem the perfect consecration to Jesus through Mary which we are now teaching them?

Sinners may say that they love Jesus, that they love and honour Mary, but they do not do so with their whole heart and soul. Unlike the elect, they do not love Jesus and Mary enough to consecrate them their body with its senses and their soul with its passions.

198. *3)* They are subject and obedient to our Lady, their good Mother, and here they are simply following the example set by our Lord himself, who spent thirty of the thirty-three years he lived on earth glorifying God his Father in perfect and entire submission to his holy Mother. They obey her, following her advice to the letter, just as Jacob followed that of Rebecca, when she said to him, *"My son, follow my advice";* or like the stewards at the wedding in Cana, to whom our Lady said, *"Do whatever he tells you."*

Through obedience to his Mother, Jacob received the blessing almost by a miracle, because in the natural course of events he should not have received it. As a reward for following the advice of our Lady, the stewards at the wedding in Cana were honoured with the first of our Lord's miracles when, at her request he changed water into wine. In the same way, until the end of time, all who are to receive the blessing of our heavenly Father and who are to be honoured with his wondrous graces will receive them only as a result of their perfect obedience to Mary. On the other hand the "Esaus" will lose their blessing because of their lack of submission to the Blessed Virgin.

199. *4)* They have great confidence in the goodness and power of the Blessed Virgin, their dear Mother, and incessantly implore her help. They take her for their pole-star to lead them safely into harbour. They open their hearts to her and tell her their troubles and their needs. They rely on her mercy and kindness to obtain forgiveness for their sins through her intercession and to experience her motherly comfort in their troubles and anxieties. They even cast themselves into her virginal bosom, hide and lose themselves there in a wonderful manner. There they are filled with pure love, they are purified from the least stain of sin, and they find Jesus in all his fulness. For he reigns in Mary as if on the most glorious of thrones. What incomparable happiness! Abbot Guerric says, "Do not imagine there is more joy in dwelling in Abraham's bosom than in Mary's, for it is in her that our Lord placed his throne."

Sinners, on the other hand, put all their confidence in themselves. Like the prodigal son, they eat with the swine. Like toads they feed on earth. Like all worldlings, they love only visible and external things. They do not know the sweetness of Mary's bosom. They do not have that reliance and confidence which the elect have for the Blessed Virgin, their Mother. Deplorably they choose to satisfy their hunger elsewhere, as St. Gregory says, because they do not want to taste the sweetness already prepared within themselves and within Jesus and Mary.

200. *5)* Finally, chosen souls keep to the ways of the Blessed Virgin, their loving Mother — that is, they imitate her and so are sincerely happy and devout and bear the infallible sign of God's chosen ones. This loving Mother says to them, "Happy are those who keep my ways",* which means, happy are those who practise my virtues and who, with the help of God's grace, follow the path of my life. They are happy in this world because of the abundance of grace and sweetness I impart to them out of my fulness, and which they receive more abundantly than others who do not imitate me so closely. They are happy at the hour of death which is sweet and peaceful for I am usually there myself to lead them home to everlasting joy. Finally, they will be happy for all eternity, because no servant of mine who imitated my virtues during life has ever been lost.

* Prov. 8:32.

On the other hand, sinners are unhappy during their life, at their death, and throughout eternity, because they do not imitate the virtues of our Lady. They are satisfied with going no further than joining her confraternities, reciting a few prayers in her honour, or performing other exterior devotional exercises.

O Blessed Virgin, my dear Mother, how happy are those who faithfully keep your ways, your counsels, and your commands; who never allow themselves to be led astray by a false devotion to you! But how unhappy and accursed are those who abuse devotion to you by not keeping the commandments of your Son. *"They are accursed who stray from your commandments."**

Services of our Lady to her faithful servants

201.   Here now are the services which the Virgin Mary, as the best of all mothers, lovingly renders to those loyal servants who have given themselves entirely to her in the manner I have described and following the figurative meaning of the story of Jacob and Rebecca.

She loves them

"I love those who love me". † She loves them:

1)   Because she is truly their Mother. What mother does not love her child, the fruit of her womb?

2)   She loves them in gratitude for the active love they show to her, their beloved Mother.

3)   She loves them because they are loved by God and destined for heaven. *"Jacob I loved but Esau I hated."* [1]

4)   She loves them because they have consecrated themselves entirely to her and belong to her portion, her inheritance. *"In Israel receive your inheritance."*

* Ps.118:21.   † Prov.8:17.   1 Rom.9:13.

202   She loves them tenderly, more tenderly than all the mothers in the world together. Take the love of all the mothers of the world for their children. Pour all that love into the heart of one mother for an only child. That mother's love would certainly be immense. Yet Mary's love for each of her children has more tenderness than the love of that mother for her child.

She loves them not only affectively but effectively, that is, her love is active and productive of good like Rebecca's love for Jacob — and even more so, for Rebecca was, after all, only a symbolic figure of Mary. Here is what this loving Mother does for her children to obtain for them the blessings of their heavenly Father:

203.   *1)*   Like Rebecca she looks out for favourable opportunities to promote their interests, to ennoble and enrich them. She sees clearly in God all that is good and all that is evil; fortunate and unfortunate events; the blessings and condemnations of God. She arranges things in advance so as to divert evils from her servants and put them in the way of abundant blessings. If there is any special benefit to be gained in God's sight by the faithful discharge of an important work, Mary will certainly obtain this opportunity for a beloved child and servant and at the same time, give him the grace to persevere in it to the end. "She personally manages our affairs," says a saintly man (Raymond Jordan).

204.   *2)*   She gives them excellent advice, as Rebecca did to Jacob. *"My son, follow my counsels."* Among other things, she persuades them to bring her the two young goats, that is, their body and soul, and to confide them to her so that she can prepare them as a dish pleasing to God. She inspires them to observe whatever Jesus Christ, her Son, has taught by word and by example. When she does not give these counsels herself in person, she gives them through the ministry of angels who are always pleased and honoured to go at her request to assist one of her faithful servants on earth.

205. *3)* What does this good Mother do when we have presented and consecrated to her our soul and body and all that pertains to them without excepting anything? Just what Rebecca of old did to the little goats Jacob brought her. *(a)* She kills them, that is, makes them die to the life of the old Adam. *(b)* She strips them of their skin, that is, of their natural inclinations, their self-love and self-will and their every attachment to creatures. *(c)* She cleanses them from all stain, impurity and sin. *(d)* She prepares them to God's taste and to his greater glory. As she alone knows perfectly what the divine taste is and where the greatest glory of God is to be found, she alone without any fear of mistake can prepare and garnish our body and soul to satisfy that infinitely refined taste and promote that infinitely hidden glory.

206. *4)* Once this good Mother has received our complete offering with our merits and satisfactions through the devotion I have been speaking about, and has stripped us of our own garments, she cleanses us and makes us worthy to appear without shame before our heavenly Father.

She clothes us in the clean, new, precious and fragrant garments of Esau, the first born, namely her Son Jesus Christ. She keeps these garments in her house, that is to say, she has them at her disposal. For she is treasurer and universal dispenser of the merits and virtues of Jesus her Son. She gives and distributes them to whom she pleases, when she pleases, as she pleases and as much as she pleases, as we have said above.

She covers the neck and hands of her servants with the skins of the goats that have been killed and flayed, that is, she adorns them with the merits and worth of their own good actions. In truth, she destroys and nullifies all that is impure and imperfect in them, but at the same time keeps the good that grace has produced in them. She preserves and enhances this good so that it adorns and strengthens their neck and hands, that is, she gives them the strength to carry the yoke of the Lord and the skill to do great things for the glory of God and the salvation of their poor brothers.

She imparts new perfume and fresh grace to those garments and adornments by adding to them the garments of her own wardrobe of merits and virtues. She bequeathed these to them before her departure for heaven, as was revealed to a holy nun of the last century, who died in the odour of sanctity. Thus all her domestics, that is, all her servants and slaves, are clothed with double garments, her own and those of her Son. Now they have nothing to fear from that cold which sinners, naked and stripped as they are of the merits of Jesus and Mary, will be unable to endure.

207. *5)* Finally, Mary obtains for them the heavenly Father's blessing. As they are the youngest born and adopted, they are not really entitled to it. Clad in new, precious, and sweet-smelling garments, with body and soul well-prepared and dressed, they confidently approach their heavenly Father. He hears their voice and recognises it as the voice of a sinner. He feels their hands covered with skins, inhales the aroma of their garments. He partakes with joy of what Mary their Mother, has prepared for him, recognizing in it the merits and good odour of his Son and his Blessed Mother.

a) He gives them a twofold blessing: the blessing of the dew of heaven,* namely divine grace, which is the seed of glory — "God has blessed us in Christ

* Gen. 27:28.

with every spiritual blessing' * — and also the blessing of the fertility of the earth, for as a provident Father, he gives them their daily bread and an ample supply of the good of the earth.

b) He makes them masters of their other brothers, the reprobate sinners. This domination does not always show in this fleeting world, where sinners often have the upper hand. "How long shall the wicked glory, mouthing insolent speeches? I have seen the wicked triumphant and lifted up like the cedars of Lebanon."† But the supremacy of the just is real and will be seen clearly for all eternity in the next world, where the just, as the Holy Spirit tells us, will dominate and command all peoples. ¹

c) The God of all majesty is not satisfied with blessing them in their persons and their possessions, he blesses all who bless them and curses all who curse and persecute them.

She provides for all their needs

208. Our Lady's charity towards her faithful servants goes further. She provides them with everything they need for body and soul. We have just seen that she gives them double garments. She also nourishes them with the most delicious food from the banquet table of God. She gives them the Son she has borne, the Bread of Life, to be their food. "Dear children," she says in the words of divine Wisdom, "take your fill of my fruit, ² that is to say, of the Fruit of Life, Jesus, whom I brought into the world for you." "Come," she repeats in another passage, "eat the bread which is Jesus. Drink the wine of his love which I have mixed for you." ³

---

* Eph.1:3.   † Ps.93:3-4;
ı Ps.36:35.   2 Ecclus.24:25. 3 Prov. 9:5. Song.5:1.

As Mary is the treasurer and dispenser of the gifts and graces of the Most High, she reserves a choice portion, indeed the choicest portion, to nourish and sustain her children and servants. They grow strong on the Bread of Life; they are made joyful with the wine that brings forth virgins.* They are carried at her breast. They bear with ease the yoke of Christ scarcely feeling its weight because of the oil of devotion with which she has softened its wood.

She leads and guides them

209.　A third service which our Lady renders her faithful servants is to lead and direct them according to the will of her Son. Rebecca guided her little son Jacob and gave him good advice from time to time, which helped him obtain the blessing of his Father and saved him from the hatred and persecution of his brother Esau. Mary, Star of the sea, guides all her faithful servants into safe harbour. She shows them the path to eternal life and helps them avoid dangerous pitfalls. She leads them by the hand along path of holiness, steadies them when they are liable to stumble and helps them rise when they have fallen. She chides them like a loving mother when they are remiss and sometimes she even lovingly chastises them. How could a child that follows such a mother and such an enlightened guide as Mary take the wrong path to heaven? Follow her and you cannot go wrong, says St. Bernard. There is no danger of a true child of Mary being led astray by the devil and falling into heresy. Where Mary leads, Satan with his deceptions and heretics with their subtleties are not encountered. "When she upholds you, you will not fall."

* Zech. 9:17.

She defends and protects them

210. The fourth good office our Lady performs for her children and faithful servants is to defend and protect them against their enemies. By her care and ingenuity Rebecca delivered Jacob from all dangers that beset him and particularly from dying at the hands of his brother, as he apparently would have done, since Esau hated and envied him just as Cain hated his brother Abel.

Mary, the beloved Mother of chosen souls, shelters them under her protecting wings as a hen does her chicks. She speaks to them, coming down to their level and accommodating herself to all their weaknesses. To ensure their safety from the hawk and vulture, she becomes their escort, surrounding them as an army in battle array. Could anyone surrounded by a well-ordered army of, say, a hundred thousand men fear his enemies? No, and still less would a faithful servant of Mary, protected on all sides by her imperial forces, fear his enemy. This powerful Queen of heaven would sooner despatch millions of angels to help one of her servants than have it said that a single faithful and trusting servant of hers had fallen victim to the malice, number and power of his enemies.

She intercedes for them

211. Finally the fifth and greatest service which this loving Mother renders her faithful followers is to intercede for them with her Son. She appeases him with her prayers, brings her servants into closest union with him and maintains that union.

Rebecca made Jacob approach the bed of his father. His father touched him, embraced him and even joyfully kissed him after having satisfied his hunger with the well-prepared dishes which Jacob had brought him. Then inhaling most joyfully the exquisite perfume of his garments, he cried: "Behold the fragrance of my son is as the fragrance of a field of plenty which the Lord has blessed." The fragrance of this rich field which so captivated the heart of the father, is none other than the fragrance of the merits and virtues of Mary, who is the plentiful field of grace in which God the Father has sown the grain of wheat of the elect, his only Son.

How welcome to Jesus Christ, the Father of the world to come, is a child perfumed with the fragrance of Mary! How readily and how intimately does he unite himself to that child! But this we have already shown at length.

212.   Furthermore, once Mary has heaped her favours upon her children and her faithful servants and has secured for them the blessing of the heavenly Father and union with Jesus Christ, she keeps them in Jesus and keeps Jesus in them. She guards them, watching over them unceasingly, lest they lose the grace of God and fall into the snares of their enemies. "She keeps the saints in their fulness" (St. Bonaventure), and inspires them to persevere to the end, as we have already said.

Such is the explanation given to this ancient allegory which typifies the mystery of predestination and reprobation.

CHAPTER SIX

WONDERFUL EFFECTS OF THIS DEVOTION

213. My dear friend, be sure that if you remain faithful to the interior and exterior practices of this devotion which I will point out, the following effects will be produced in your soul:

1. Knowledge of our unworthiness

By the light which the Holy Spirit will give you through Mary, his faithful spouse, you will perceive the evil inclinations of your fallen nature and how incapable you are of any good apart from that which God produces in you as Author of nature and of grace. As a consequence of this knowledge you will despise yourself and think of yourself only as an object of repugnance. You will consider yourself as a snail that soils everything with its slime, as a toad that poisons everything with its venom, as a malevolent serpent seeking only to deceive. Finally, the humble Virgin Mary will share her humility with you so that, although you regard yourself with distaste and desire to be disregarded by others, you will not look down slightingly upon anyone.

2. A Share in Mary's Faith

214. Mary will share her faith with you. Her faith on earth was stronger than that of all the patriarchs, prophets, apostles and saints. Now that she is reigning in heaven she no longer has this faith, since she sees everything clearly in God by the light of glory. However, with the consent of Almighty God she did not lose it when entering heaven. She has preserved it for her faithful servants in the Church Militant. Therefore the more you gain the friendship of this noble Queen and Virgin, the more will you be inspired by faith in your daily life. It will cause you to depend less upon sensible and extraordinary feelings. For it is a lively faith animated by charity enabling you to do everything from no other motive than that of pure love.* It is a firm faith, unshakeable as a rock, prompting you to remain firm and steadfast in the midst of storms and tempests. It is an active and probing faith which like some mysterious pass-key admits you into the mysteries of Jesus Christ and of man's final destiny and into the very heart of God himself. It is a courageous faith which inspires you to undertake and carry out without hesitation great things for God and the salvation of souls. Lastly, this faith will be your flaming torch, your very life with God your secret fund of divine Wisdom, and an all-powerful weapon for you to enlighten those who sit in darkness and the shadow of death. It inflames those who are lukewarm and need the gold of fervent love. It restores life to those who are dead through sin. It moves and transforms hearts of marble and cedars of Lebanon by gentle and convincing argument. Finally, this faith will strengthen you to resist the devil and the other enemies of salvation.

3. The gift of pure love

215. The Mother of fair love will rid your heart of all scruples and inordinate servile fear. She will open and enlarge it to obey the commandments of her Son with alacrity and with the holy freedom of the children of God. She will fill your heart with pure love of which she is the treasury. You will then cease to act, as you did before, out of fear of God who is love, but rather out of pure love. You will look upon him as a loving Father

---

* This number is filled with biblical allusion: Gal.5:6; Col.1:23; Rom.5:1-2; Heb.11:33; Col.2:3; Lk.1:79; 1 Pet.5:8-9.

and endeavour to please him at all times. You will speak trustfully to him as a child does to its father. If you should have the misfortune to offend him you will abase yourself before him and humbly beg his pardon. You will offer your hand to him with simplicity and lovingly rise from your sin. Then, peaceful and relaxed and buoyed up with hope, you will continue on your way to him.

4. Great confidence in God and in Mary

216.   Our Blessed Lady will fill you with unbounded confidence in God and in herself:

1)   Because you will no longer approach Jesus by yourself but always through Mary your loving Mother.

2)   Since you have given her all your merits, graces and satisfactions to dispose of as she pleases, she imparts to you her own virtues and clothes you in her own merits. So you will be able to say confidently to God, "Behold Mary, your handmaid, be it done unto me according to your word."

3)   Since you have now given yourself completely to Mary, body and soul, she, who is generous to the generous, and more generous than even the kindest benefactor, will in return give herself to you in a marvellous but real manner. Indeed you may without hesitation say to her, "I am yours, O Blessed Virgin, obtain salvation for me",* or with the beloved disciple, St. John, "I have taken you, Blessed Mother, for my all." Or again you may say with St. Bonaventure, "Dear Mother of saving grace, I will do everything with confidence and without fear because you are my strength and my boast in the Lord," or in another place, "I am yours and all that I have is yours, O glorious Virgin, blessed above all created things. Let me place you as a

*   Cf.Ps.118:94.

seal upon my heart, for your love is as strong as death." Or adopting the sentiments of the prophet, "Lord, my heart has no reason to be exalted nor should my looks be proud; I have not sought things of great moment nor wonders beyond my reach, nevertheless, I still am not humble. But I have roused my soul and taken courage. I am as a child, weaned from earthly pleasures and resting on its mother's breast. It is upon this breast that all good things come to me."*

4) What will still further increase your confidence in her is that, after having given her in trust all that you possess to use or keep as she pleases, you will place less trust in yourself and much more in her whom you have made your treasury. How comforting and how consoling when a person can say that the treasury of God, where he has placed all that he holds most precious, is also his treasury. "She is," says a saintly man, "the treasury of the Lord."

5. Communication of the spirit of Mary

217. The soul of Mary will be communicated to you to glorify the Lord. Her spirit will take the place of yours to rejoice in God, her Saviour, but only if you are faithful to the practices of this devotion. As St. Ambrose says, May the soul of Mary be in each one of us to glorify the Lord! May the spirit of Mary be in each one of us to rejoice in God! "When will that happy day come," asks a saintly man of our own day whose life was completely wrapped up in Mary, "when God's Mother is enthroned in men's hearts as Queen, subjecting them to the dominion of her great and princely Son. When will souls breathe Mary as the body breathes air?"

When that time comes wonderful things will

---

*   Cf. Ps.130:1-2.

happen on earth. The Holy Spirit, finding his dear Spouse present again in souls, will come down into them with great power. He will fill them with his gifts, especially wisdom, by which they will produce wonders of grace. My dear friend, when will that happy time come, that age of Mary, when many souls, chosen by Mary and given her by the most High God, will hide themselves completely in the depths of her soul, becoming living copies of her, loving and glorifying Jesus. That day will dawn only when the devotion I teach is understood and put into practice. *Ut adveniat regnum tuum, adveniat regnum Mariae.* "Lord, that your kingdom may come, may the reign of Mary come!"

6. Transformation into the likeness of Jesus

218. If Mary, the Tree of Life, is well cultivated in our soul by fidelity to this devotion, she will in due time bring forth her fruit, which is none other than Jesus. I have seen many devout souls searching for Jesus in one way or another, and so often when they have worked hard throughout the night, all they can say is, "Despite our having worked all night, we have caught nothing."* To them we can say, "You have worked hard and gained little:† Jesus can only be recognised faintly in you." But if we follow the immaculate path of Mary, living the devotion that I teach, we will always work in daylight, we will work in a holy place, and we will work but little. There is no darkness in Mary, not even the slightest shadow since there was never any sin in her. She is a holy place, a holy of holies, in which saints are formed and moulded.

219. Please note that I say that saints are moulded in Mary. There is a vast difference between carving a statue by blows of hammer and chisel and making a

* Lk. 5:5.   † Hag. 1:6.

statue by using a mould. Sculptors and statue-makers work hard and need plenty of time to make statues by the first method. But the second method does not involve much work and takes very little time. St. Augustine speaking to our Blessed Lady says, *"You are worthy to be called the mould of God."* Mary is a mould capable of forming people into the image of the God-man. Anyone who is cast into this divine mould is quickly shaped and moulded into Jesus and Jesus into him. At little cost and in a short time he will become Christ-like since he is cast into the very same mould that fashioned a God-man.

220.   I think I can very well compare to sculptors some spiritual directors and devout persons who wish to produce Jesus in themselves and in others by methods other than this. Many of them rely on their own skill, ingenuity and art, and chip away endlessly with mallet and chisel at hard stone or badly-prepared wood, in an effort to produce a likeness of our Lord. At times, they do not manage to produce a recognisable likeness either because they lack knowledge and experience of the person of Jesus or because a clumsy stroke has spoiled the whole work. But those who accept this little known secret of grace which I offer them can rightly be compared to smelters and moulders who have discovered the beautiful mould of Mary where Jesus was so divinely and so naturally formed.*

They do not rely on their own skill but on the perfection of the mould. They cast and lose themselves in Mary where they become true models of her Son.

221.   You may think this is a beautiful and convincing comparison. But how many understand it? I would like you, my dear friend, to understand it. But remember

---

* "Naturally", that is, in human nature and by voluntary colla-boration. "Divinely", that is, by the operation of the Holy Spirit.

that only molten and liquified substances may be poured into a mould. That means that you must crush and melt down the old Adam in you if you wish to acquire the likeness of the new Adam in Mary.

7. The greater glory of Christ

222. If you live this devotion sincerely, you will give more glory to Jesus in a month than in many years of a more demanding devotion. Here are my reasons for saying this:

1) Since you do everything through the Blessed Virgin as required by this devotion, you naturally lay aside your own intentions no matter how good they appear to you. You abandon yourself to our Lady's intentions even though you do not know what they are. Thus you share in the high quality of her intentions which are so pure that she gave more glory to God by the smallest of her actions, say, twirling her distaff or making a stitch, than did St. Laurence suffering his cruel martyrdom on the grid-iron, and even more than all the saints together in all their most heroic deeds! Mary amassed such a multitude of merits and graces during her sojourn on earth that it would be easier to count the stars in heaven, the drops of water in the ocean or the sands of the sea-shore than count her merits and graces. She thus gave more glory to God than all the angels and saints have given or will ever give him. Mary, wonder of God, when souls abandon themselves to you, you cannot but work wonders in them!

223. *2)* In this devotion we set no store on our own thoughts and actions but are content to rely on Mary's dispositions when approaching and even speaking to Jesus. We then act with far greater humility than others who, imperceptibly, rely on their own dispositions and are self-satisfied about them; and consequently we give greater glory to God, for perfect glory is given to him only by the lowly and humble of heart.

224. *3)* Our Blessed Lady, in her immense love for us, is eager to receive into her virginal hands the gift of our actions, imparting to them a marvellous beauty and splendour, and presenting them herself to Jesus most willingly. More glory is given to our Lord in this way than when we make our offering with our own guilty hands.

225. *4)* Lastly, you never think of Mary without Mary thinking of God for you. You never praise or honour Mary without Mary joining you in praising and honouring God. Mary is entirely relative to God. Indeed I would say that she was relative only to God, because she exists uniquely in reference to him. She is an echo of God, speaking and repeating only *God.* If you say "Mary" she says "God". When St. Elizabeth praised Mary calling her blessed because she had believed, Mary, the faithful echo of God, responded with her Canticle, "My soul glorifies the Lord." What Mary did on that day, she does every day. When we praise her, when we love and honour her, when we present anything to her, then God is praised, honoured and loved, and receives our gift through Mary and in Mary.

CHAPTER SEVEN

PARTICULAR PRACTICES OF THIS DEVOTION

1. EXTERIOR PRACTICES

226. Although this devotion is essentially an interior one, that does not prevent it from having exterior practices which should not be neglected. "These must be done but those not omitted."* If properly performed exterior acts help to foster interior ones. Man is always guided by his senses, and such practices remind him of what he has done or should do. Let no worldling or critic intervene to assert that true devotion is essentially in the heart and therefore externals should be avoided as inspiring vanity, or that real devotion should be hidden and private. I answer in the words of our Lord, "Let man see your good works that they may glorify your Father who is in heaven." As St. Gregory says, this does not mean that they should perform external actions to please men or to seek praise; that certainly would be vanity. It simply means that we do these things before men only to please and glorify God without worrying about either the contempt or the approval of men.

I shall briefly mention some practices which I call exterior, not because they are performed without inner attention but because they have an exterior element as distinct from those which are purely interior.

1) Preparation and Consecration

227. Those who wish to take up this special devotion, (which has not been erected into a confraternity, although this would be desirable†), should spend at least

---

* Mt.23:23.

† In 1899, the first Confraternity of Mary, Queen of our Hearts, was erected in Ottawa. In 1913, Pius X erected the confraternity in Rome into an Archconfraternity. In 1955, the Holy See established two distinct associations, for the faithful and for priests. The association for the faithful possesses today 140 centres spread throughout the world. For centres in Great Britain see end of book.

twelve days in emptying themselves of the spirit of the world, which is opposed to the spirit of Jesus, as I have recommended in the first part of this preparation for the reign of Jesus Christ. Then they should spend three weeks imbuing themselves with the spirit of Jesus through the most Blessed Virgin. Here is a programme they might follow:

228. During the first week they should offer up all their prayers and acts of devotion to acquire knowledge of themselves and sorrow for their sins.

Let them perform all their actions in a spirit of humility. With this end in view they may, if they wish, meditate on what I have said concerning our corrupted nature and consider themselves during six days of the week as nothing but snails, slugs, toads, swine, snakes and goats. Or else they may meditate on the following three considerations of St. Bernard: *"Remember what you were — corrupted seed, what you are — a body destined for decay; what you will be — food for worms."*

They will ask our Lord and the Holy Spirit to enlighten them saying "Lord, that I may see", or "Lord, let me know myself", or the "Come Holy Spirit". Every day they should say the Litany of the Holy Spirit, with the prayer that follows, as indicated in the first part of this work. They will turn to our Blessed Lady and beg her to obtain for them that great grace which is the foundation of all others, the grace of self-knowledge. For this intention they will say each day the *Ave Maris Stella* and the Litany of the Blessed Virgin.

229. Each day of the second week they should endeavour in all their prayers and works to acquire an understanding of the Blessed Virgin and ask the Holy Spirit for this grace. They may read and meditate on what we have already said about her. They should recite daily the Litany of the Holy Spirit and the *Ave*

Maris Stella as during the first week. In addition they will say at least five decades of the Rosary for greater understanding of Mary.

230.   During the third week they should seek to under-stand Jesus Christ better. They may read and meditate on what we have already said about him. They may say the prayer of St. Augustine which they will find at the beginning of the second part of this book. Again with St. Augustine, they may pray repeatedly, *"Lord, that I may know you"*, or *"Lord, that I may see"*. As during the previous week, they should recite the Litany of the Holy Spirit and the *Ave Maris Stella,* adding every day the Litany of the Holy Name of Jesus.

231.   At the end of these three weeks they should go to confession and Holy Communion with the intention of consecrating themselves to Jesus through Mary as his slaves of love. When receiving Holy Communion they could follow the method given later on. They then re-cite the act of consecration which is given at the end of this book. If they do not have a printed copy of the act, they should write it out or have it copied and then sign it on the very day they make it.

232.   It would be very becoming if on that day they offered some tribute to Jesus and his Mother, either as a penance for past unfaithfulness to the promises made in baptism or as a sign of their submission to the sover-eignty of Jesus and Mary. Such a tribute would be in accordance with each one's ability and fervour and may take the form of fasting, an act of self-denial, the gift of an alms or the offering of a votive candle. If they gave only a pin as a token of their homage, provided it were given with a good heart, it would satisfy Jesus who considers only the good intention.

233.   Every year at least, on the same date, they should renew the consecration following the same exercises for three weeks. They might also renew it every month or even every day by saying this short prayer: "I am all yours and all I have is yours, O dear Jesus, through Mary, your holy Mother."

2) The Little Crown of the Blessed Virgin

234. If it is not too inconvenient, they should recite every day of their lives the Little Crown of the Blessed Virgin, which is composed of three Our Fathers and twelve Hail Marys in honour of the twelve glorious privileges of Mary. This prayer is very old and is based on Holy Scripture. St. John saw in a vision a woman crowned with twelve stars, clothed with the sun and standing upon the moon.* According to biblical commentators, this woman is the Blessed Virgin.

235. There are several ways of saying the Little Crown but it would take too long to explain them here. The Holy Spirit will teach them to those who live this devotion conscientiously. However, here is a simple way to recite it. As an introduction say, "Virgin most holy, accept my praise; give me strength to fight your foes", then say the Creed. Next, say the following sequence of prayers three times: one Our Father, four Hail Marys and one Glory be to the Father. In conclusion say the prayer, *Sub tuum,* "We fly to thy patronage."

3) The Wearing of Little Chains

236. It is very praiseworthy and helpful for those who have become slaves of Jesus in Mary to wear, in token of their slavery of love, a little chain blessed with a special blessing.† It is perfectly true these external tokens are not essential and may very well be dispensed with by those who have made this consecration. Never-

---

* Apoc.12:1.

† Nowadays, the chain is usually worn round the neck with a Medal of our Lady, e.g. the Confraternity medal.

theless, I cannot help but give the warmest approval to those who wear them. They show they have shaken off the shameful chains of the slavery of the devil, in which original sin and perhaps actual sin had bound them, and have willingly taken upon themselves the glorious slavery of Jesus Christ. Like St. Paul, they glory in the chains they wear for Christ. For though these chains are made only of iron they are far more glorious and precious than all the gold ornaments worn by monarchs.

237. At one time, nothing was considered more contemptible than the Cross. Now this sacred wood has become the most glorious symbol of the Christian faith. Similarly, nothing was more ignoble in the sight of the ancients, and even today nothing is more degrading among unbelievers than the chains of Jesus Christ, but among Christians nothing is more glorious than these chains, because by them Christians are liberated and kept free from the ignoble shackles of sin and the devil. Thus set free, we are bound to Jesus and Mary not by compulsion and force like galley-slaves, but by charity and love as children are to their parents. *"I shall draw them to me by chains of love"* said God Most High speaking through the prophet.* Consequently, these chains are as strong as death, and in a way stronger than death, for those who wear them faithfully till the end of their life. For though death destroys and corrupts their body, it will not destroy the chains of their slavery, since these, being of metal, will not easily corrupt. It may be that on the day of their resurrection, that momentous day of final judgement, these chains still clinging to their bones, will contribute to their glorification and be transformed into chains of light and splendour. Happy then, a thousand times happy, are the illustrious slaves of Jesus in Mary who bear their chains even to the grave.

* Hos. 11:4.

238.   Here are the reasons for wearing these chains:

   a)   They remind a Christian of the promises of his baptism and the perfect renewal of these commitments made in his consecration. They remind him of his strict obligation to adhere faithfully to them. A man's actions are prompted more frequently by his senses than by pure faith and so he can easily forget his duties towards God if he has no external reminder of them. These little chains are a wonderful aid in recalling the bonds of sin and the slavery of the devil from which baptism has freed him. At the same time, they remind him of the dependence on Jesus promised at baptism and ratified when by consecration he renewed these promises. Why is it that so many Christians do not think of their baptismal vows and behave with as much licence as unbelievers who have promised nothing to God? One explanation is that they do not wear external signs to remind them of these vows.

239.   *b)*   These chains prove they are not ashamed of being the servants and slaves of Jesus and that they reject the deadly bondage of the world, of sin and of the devil.

   c)   They are a guarantee and protection against enslavement by sin and the devil. For we must of necessity choose to wear either the chains of sin and damnation or the chains of love and salvation.

240.   Dear friend, break the chains of sin and of sinners, of the world and the worldly, of the devil and his satellites. "Cast their yoke of death far from us."* To use the words of the Holy Spirit, let us put our feet into his glorious shackles and our neck into his chains. Let us bow down our shoulders in submission to the yoke of Wisdom incarnate, Jesus Christ, and let us not be upset by the burden of his chains. Notice how before

   *   Ps. 2:3.

saying these words the Holy Spirit prepares us to accept his serious advice, "Hearken, my son," he says, "receive a counsel of understanding and do not spurn this counsel of mine."*

241. Allow me here, my dear friend, to join the Holy Spirit in giving you the same counsel. "These chains are the chains of salvation."† As our Lord on the Cross draws all men to himself, whether they will it or not, he will draw sinners by the fetters of their sins and submit them like galley-slaves and devils to his eternal anger and avenging justice. But he will draw the just, especially in these latter days, by the chains of love.

242. These loving slaves of Christ may wear their chains around the neck, on their arms, round the waist or round the ankles. Father Vincent Caraffa, seventh General of the Society of Jesus, who died in the odour of sanctity in 1643, carried an iron band round his ankles as a symbol of his holy servitude and he used to say that his greatest regret was that he could not drag a chain around in public. Mother Agnes of Jesus, of whom we have already spoken, wore a chain around her waist. Others have worn it round the neck, in atonement for the pearl necklaces they wore in the world. Others have worn chains round their arms to remind them, as they worked with their hands, that they are the slaves of Jesus.

4) Honouring the mystery of the Incarnation

243. Loving slaves of Jesus in Mary should hold in high esteem devotion to Jesus, the Word of God, in the great mystery of the Incarnation, March 25th, which is the mystery proper to this devotion, because it was inspired by the Holy Spirit for the following reasons:

        a) That we might honour and imitate the

---

* Ecclus. 6:25,24,26.   † Ecclus. 6:31.

wondrous dependence which God the Son chose to have on Mary, for the glory of his Father and for the redemption of man. This dependence is revealed especially in this mystery where Jesus becomes a slave in the womb of his Blessed Mother, depending on her for everything.

b) That we might thank God for the incomparable graces he has conferred upon Mary and especially that of choosing her to be his most worthy Mother. This choice was made in the mystery of the Incarnation. These are the two principal ends of the slavery of Jesus in Mary.

244. Please note that I usually say "slave of Jesus in Mary," "slavery of Jesus in Mary". We might say, as some have already been saying, "slave of Mary", "slavery of Mary". But I think it preferable to say, "slave of Jesus in Mary". This is the opinion of Father Tronson, Superior General of the Seminary of St. Sulpice, a man renowned for his exceptional prudence and remarkable holiness. He gave this advice when consulted upon this subject by a priest.

Here are the reasons for it:

245. *a)* Since we live in an age of pride when a great number of haughty scholars, with proud and critical minds, find fault even with long-established and sound devotions, it is better to speak of "slavery of Jesus in Mary" and to call oneself "slave of Jesus" rather than "slave of Mary". We then avoid giving any pretext for criticism. In this way, we name this devotion after its ultimate end which is Jesus, rather than after the way and the means to arrive there, which is Mary. However we can very well use either term without any scruple, as I myself do. If a man goes from Orleans to Tours, by way of Amboise, he can quite truthfully say that he is going to Tours. The only difference is that Amboise is simply a place on the direct road to Tours, and Tours alone is his final destination.

246. *b)* Since the principal mystery celebrated and honoured in this devotion is the mystery of the Incarnation where we find Jesus only in Mary, having become incarnate in her womb, it is more appropriate for us to say, "slavery of Jesus in Mary," of Jesus dwelling enthroned in Mary, according to the beautiful prayer, recited by so many great souls, "O Jesus, living in Mary."*

247. *c)* These expressions show more clearly the intimate union existing between Jesus and Mary. So closely are they united that one is wholly in the other. Jesus is all in Mary and Mary is all in Jesus. Or rather, it is no longer she who lives, but Jesus alone who lives in her. It would be easier to separate light from the sun than Mary from Jesus. So united are they, that our Lord may be called "Jesus of Mary", and his Mother "Mary of Jesus".

248. Time does not permit me to linger here and elaborate on the perfections and wonders of the mystery of Jesus living and reigning in Mary, or the Incarnation of the Word. I shall confine myself to the following brief remarks. The Incarnation is the first mystery of Jesus Christ; it is the most hidden; and it is the most exalted and the least known.

It was in this mystery that Jesus, in the womb of Mary and with her co-operation, chose all the elect. For this reason that the saints called her womb the throne-room of God's mysteries.

It was in this mystery that Jesus anticipated all subsequent mysteries of his life by his willing accept-

---

* This is the complete prayer: "O Jesus living in Mary, come and dwell in your servants in the spirit of your holiness, in the fulness of your power, in the perfection of your ways, in the truth of your virtues, in the communion of your mysteries. Subdue our enemies, the world and the flesh, in the strength of your Spirit, for the glory of your Father. Amen.

ance of them. Consequently, this mystery is a summary of all his mysteries since it contains the intention and the grace of them all.

Lastly, this mystery is the seat of the mercy, the liberality, and the glory of God. It is the seat of his *mercy* for us, since we can approach and speak to Jesus through Mary. We need her intervention to see or speak to him. Here, ever responsive to the prayer of his Mother, Jesus unfailingly grants grace and mercy to all poor sinners. "Let us come boldly then before the throne of grace."*

It is the seat of *liberality* for Mary, because while the new Adam dwelt in this truly earthly paradise, God performed there so many hidden marvels beyond the understanding of men and angels. For this reason, the saints call Mary "the magnificence of God," as if God showed his magnificence only in Mary. It is the seat of *glory* for his Father, because it was in Mary that Jesus perfectly atoned to his Father on behalf of mankind. It was here that he perfectly restored the glory that sin had taken from his Father. It was here again that our Lord, by the sacrifice of himself and of his will, gave more glory to God than he would have given had he offered all the sacrifices of the Old Law. Finally, in Mary he gave his Father infinite glory, such as his Father had never received from man.

5) Saying the Hail Mary and the Rosary

249. Those who accept this devotion should have a great love for the Hail Mary, or, as it is called, the Angelic Salutation.

Few Christians however enlightened, understand the value, merit, excellence and necessity of the Hail Mary. Our Blessed Lady herself had to appear on several

* Heb.4:16.

occasions to men of great holiness and insight, such as St. Dominic, St. John Capistran and Blessed Alan de Rupe, to convince them of the richness of this prayer.

They composed whole books on the wonders it had worked and its efficacy in converting sinners. They earnestly proclaimed and publicly preached that just as the salvation of the world began with the Hail Mary, so the salvation of each individual is bound up with it. This prayer, they said, brought to a dry and barren world the Fruit of Life, and if well said, will cause the Word of God to take root in the soul and bring forth Jesus, the Fruit of Life. They also tell us that the Hail Mary is a heavenly dew which waters the earth of our soul and makes it bear its fruit in due season. The soul which is not watered by this heavenly dew bears no fruit but only thorns and briars, and merits only God's condemnation.

250. Here is what our Blessed Lady revealed to Blessed Alan de Rupe as recorded in his book, "The Dignity of the Rosary", and as told again by Cartagena: "Know, my son, and make it known to all, that luke-warmness or negligence in saying the Hail Mary, or a distaste for it, is a probable and proximate sign of eternal damnation, for by this prayer the whole world was restored."

These are terrible words but at the same time they are consoling. We should find it hard to believe them, were we not assured of their truth by Blessed Alan and by St. Dominic before him, and by so many great men since his time. The experience of many centuries is there to prove it, for it has always been common knowledge that those who bear the sign of reprobation, as all formal heretics, evil-doers, the proud and the worldly, hate and spurn the Hail Mary and the Rosary. True, heretics learn to say the Our Father but they will not countenance the Hail Mary and the Rosary and they would rather carry a snake around with them than a rosary. And there are even Catholics, who, sharing the proud tendencies of their father Lucifer, despise the Hail Mary or look upon it with indifference. The Rosary, they say, is a devotion suitable only for ignorant and illiterate people.

On the other hand, we know from experience that those who show positive signs of being among the elect, appreciate and love the Hail Mary and are always glad to say it. The closer they are to God, the more they love this prayer, as our Blessed Lady went on to tell Blessed Alan.

251. I do not know how this should be, but it is perfectly true; and I know no surer way of discovering whether a person belongs to God than by finding out if he loves saying the Hail Mary and the Rosary. I say, "if he loves", for it can happen that a person for some reason may be unable to say the Rosary, but this does not prevent him from loving it and inspiring others to say it.

252. Chosen souls, slaves of Jesus in Mary, understand that after the Our Father, the Hail Mary is the most beautiful of all prayers. It is the perfect compliment the most high God paid to Mary through his archangel in order to win her heart. So powerful was the effect of this greeting upon her, on account of its hidden delights, that despite her great humility, she gave her consent to the incarnation of the Word. If you say the Hail Mary properly, this compliment will infallibly earn you Mary's good will.

253. When the Hail Mary is well said, that is, with attention, devotion and humility, it is, according to the saints, the enemy of Satan, putting him to flight; it is the hammer that crushes him, a source of holiness for souls, a joy to the angels and a sweet melody for the devout. It is the Canticle of the New Testament, a delight for Mary and glory for the most Blessed Trinity. The Hail Mary is dew falling from heaven to make the soul fruitful. It is a pure kiss of love we give to Mary. It is a crimson rose, a precious pearl that we offer to her. It is a cup of ambrosia, of divine nectar that we give her. These are comparisons made by the saints.

254. I earnestly beg of you, then, by the love I bear you in Jesus and Mary, not to be content with saying the Little Crown of the Blessed Virgin, but say the Rosary too, and if time permits, all its fifteen decades, every day. Then when death draws near, you will bless the day and hour when you took to heart what I told you, for having sown the blessings of Jesus and Mary, you will reap eternal blessings in heaven.[*]

6) Praying the Magnificat

255. To thank God for the graces he has given to our Lady, her consecrated ones will frequently say the *Magnificat,* following the example of Blessed Marie d'Oignies and several other saints. The *Magnificat* is the only prayer we have which was composed by our Lady, or rather, composed by Jesus in her, for it was he who spoke through her lips. It is the greatest offering of praise that God ever received under the law of grace. On the one hand, it is the most humble hymn of thanksgiving, and on the other, it is the most sublime and exalted. Contained in it are mysteries so great and so hidden that even the angels do not understand them.

Gerson, a pious and learned scholar, spent the greater part of his life writing tracts full of erudition and love on the most profound subjects. Even so, it was with apprehension that he undertook, towards the end

[*] Cf.2 Cor.9:6.

of his life, to write a commentary on the *Magnificat* which was the crowning point of all his works. In a large volume on the subject he says many wonderful things about this beautiful and divine canticle. Among other things he tells us that Mary herself frequently recited it, especially as thanks-giving after Holy Communion. The learned Benzonius, in his commentary on the *Magnificat,* cites several miracles worked through the power of this prayer. The devils, he declares, take to flight when they hear these words, "He puts forth his arm in strength and scatters the proud-hearted."

7) Contempt of the world

256. Mary's faithful servants must despise this corrupted world. They should hate and shun its allurements, and follow the exercises of the contempt of the world which we have given in the first part of this treatise.

2. SPECIAL INTERIOR PRACTICES FOR THOSE WHO WISH TO BE PERFECT

257. The exterior practices of this devotion which I have just dealt with should be observed as far as one's circumstances and state of life permit. They should not be omitted through negligence or deliberate disregard. In addition to them, here are some very sanctifying interior practices for those souls who feel called by the Holy Spirit to a high degree of perfection. They may be expressed in four words, doing everything THROUGH Mary, WITH Mary, IN Mary and FOR Mary, in order to do them more perfectly *through* Jesus, *with* Jesus, *in* Jesus and *for* Jesus.

Through Mary

258. We must do everything through Mary, that is,

we must obey her always and be led in all things by her spirit, which is the Holy Spirit of God. "Those who are led by the Spirit of God are children of God," says St. Paul.* Those who are led by the spirit of Mary are children of Mary, and, consequently children of God, as we have already shown. Among the many servants of Mary only those who are truly and faithfully devoted to her are led by her spirit.

I have said that the spirit of Mary is the spirit of God because she was never led by her own spirit, but always by the spirit of God, who made himself master of her to such an extent that he became her very spirit. That is why St. Ambrose says, "May the spirit of Mary be in each one of us to rejoice in God." Happy is the man who follows the example of the good Jesuit Brother Rodriguez, who died in the odour of sanctity, because he will be completely possessed and governed by the spirit of Mary, a spirit which is gentle yet strong, zealous yet prudent, humble yet courageous, pure yet fruitful.

259. The person who wishes to be led by this spirit of Mary

1) Should renounce his own spirit, his own views and his own will before doing anything, for example, before making meditation, celebrating or attending Mass, before Communion. For the darkness of our own spirit and the evil tendencies of our own will and actions, good as they may seem to us, would hinder the holy spirit of Mary were we to follow them.

2) We should give ourselves up to the spirit of Mary to be moved and directed as she wishes. We should place and leave ourselves in her virginal hands, like a tool in the hands of a craftsman or a lute in the hands of a good musician. We should cast ourselves into her

* Rom. 8:14.

like a stone thrown into the sea. This is done easily and quickly by a mere thought, a slight movement of the will or just a few words as — "I renounce myself and give myself to you, my dear Mother." And even if we do not experience any emotional fervour in this spiritual encounter, it is none the less real. It is just as if a person with equal sincerity were to say — which God forbid! — "I give myself to the devil." Even though this were said without feeling any emotion, he would no less really belong to the devil.

3) From time to time during an action and after it, we should renew this same act of offering and of union. The more we do so, the quicker we shall grow in holiness and the sooner we shall reach union with Christ, which necessarily follows upon union with Mary, since the spirit of Mary is the spirit of Jesus.

With Mary

260. We must do everything with Mary, that is to say, in all our actions we must look upon Mary, although a simple human being, as the perfect model of every virtue and perfection, fashioned by the Holy Spirit for us to imitate, as far as our limited capacity allows. In every action then we should consider how Mary performed it or how she would perform it if she were in our place. For this reason, we must examine and meditate on the great virtues she practised during her life, especially:

1) Her lively faith, by which she believed the angel's word without the least hesitation, and believed faithfully and constantly even to the foot of the Cross on Calvary.

2) Her deep humility, which made her prefer seclusion, maintain silence, submit to every eventuality and put herself in the last place.

3) Her truly divine purity, which never had and never will have its equal on this side of heaven.

And so on for her other virtues.

Remember what I told you before, that Mary is the great, unique mould of God, designed to make living images of God at little cost and in a short time. Anyone who finds this mould and casts himself into it, is soon transformed into our Lord because it is the true likeness of him.

In Mary

261. We must do everything in Mary. To understand this we must realise that the Blessed Virgin is the true earthly paradise of the new Adam and that the ancient paradise was only a symbol of her.* There are in this earthly paradise untold riches, beauties, rarities and delights, which the new Adam, Jesus Christ, has left there. It is in this paradise that he took his delights for nine months, worked his wonders and displayed his riches with the magnificence of God himself. This most holy place consists of only virgin and immaculate soil from which the new Adam was formed with neither spot nor stain by the operation of the Holy Spirit who dwells there. In this earthly paradise grows the real Tree of Life which bore our Lord, the fruit of Life, and the Tree of knowledge of good and evil, which bore the Light of the world.

In this divine place there are trees planted by the hand of God and watered by his divine unction which have borne and continue to bear fruit that is pleasing to him. There are flowerbeds studded with a variety of beautiful flowers of virtue, diffusing a fragrance which delights even the angels. Here there are meadows verdant with hope, impregnable towers of

* The whole of this number is a commentary on Gen. 2: 8-10, on the earthly paradise.

fortitude, enchanting mansions of confidence, and many other delights.

Only the Holy Spirit can teach us the truths that these material objects symbolise. In this place the air is perfectly pure. There is no night, but only the brilliant day of the sacred humanity, the resplendent, spotless sun of the Divinity, the blazing furnace of love, melting all the base metal thrown into it and changing it into gold. There the river of humility gushes forth from the soil, divides into four branches and irrigates the whole of this enchanted place. These branches are the four cardinal virtues.

262.   The Holy Spirit speaking through the Fathers of the Church, also calls our Lady the Eastern Gate, through which the High Priest, Jesus Christ, enters and goes out into the world.* Through this gate he entered the world the first time and through this same gate he will come the second time.

The Holy Spirit also calls her the Sanctuary of the Divinity, the Resting-place of the Holy Trinity, the Throne of God, the City of God, the Altar of God, the Temple of God, the World of God. All these titles and expressions of praise are very real when related to the different wonders the Almighty worked in her and the graces which he bestowed on her. What wealth and what glory! What a joy and a privilege for us to enter and dwell in Mary, in whom almighty God has set up the throne of his supreme glory!

263.   But how difficult it is for us sinners to have the freedom, the ability and the light to enter such an exalted and holy place. This place is guarded not by a cherub, like the first earthly paradise, but by the Holy Spirit himself who has become its absolute Master. Referring to her, he says, "You are an enclosed garden,

* Ezek.44:1-3.

my bride, an enclosed garden and a sealed fountain."* Mary is enclosed. Mary is sealed. The unfortunate children of Adam and Eve, driven from the earthly paradise, can enter this new paradise only by a special grace of the Holy Spirit which they have to merit.

264. When we have obtained this remarkable grace by our fidelity, we should be delighted to remain in Mary. We should rest there peacefully, rely on her confidently, hide ourselves there with safety, and abandon ourselves unconditionally to her, so that within her virginal bosom:

1) We may be nourished with the milk of her grace and her motherly compassion.

2) We may be delivered from all anxiety, fear and scruples.

3) We may be safeguarded from all our enemies, the devil, the world and sin which have never gained admittance there. That is why our Lady says that those who work in her will not sin, that is, those who dwell spiritually in our Lady will never commit serious sin.

4) We may be formed in our Lord and our Lord formed in us, because her womb is, as the early Fathers call it, the house of the divine secrets where Jesus and all the elect have been conceived. "This one and that one were born in her."

For Mary

265. Finally we must do everything for Mary. Since we have given ourselves completely to her service, it is only right that we should do everything for her as if we were her personal servant and slave. This does not mean that we take her for the ultimate end of our service, for Jesus alone is our ultimate end. But we take Mary for

* Song of Songs, 4:12.

our proximate end, our mysterious intermediary and the easiest way of reaching him.

Like every good servant and slave we must not remain idle, but, relying on her protection, we should undertake and carry out great things for our noble Queen. We must defend her privileges when they are questioned and uphold her good name when it is under attack. We must attract everyone, if possible, to her service and to this true and sound devotion. We must speak up and denounce those who distort devotion to her by outraging her Son, and at the same time we must apply ourselves to spreading this true devotion. As a reward for these little services, we should expect nothing in return save the honour of belonging to such a lovable Queen and the joy of being united through her to Jesus, her Son, by a bond that is indissoluble in time and in eternity. Glory to Jesus in Mary! Glory to Mary in Jesus! Glory to God alone!

THIS DEVOTION AT HOLY COMMUNION

Before Holy Communion

266. *1)* Place yourself humbly in the presence of God.

2) Renounce your corrupt nature and dispositions, no matter how good self-love makes them appear
to you.

3) Renew your consecration saying, "I belong
entirely to you, dear Mother, and all that I have is yours."

4) Implore Mary to lend you her heart so that
you may receive her Son with her dispositions. Remind
her that her Son's glory requires that he should not
come into a heart so sullied and so fickle as your own,
which could not fail to diminish his glory and might
cause him to leave. Tell her that if she will take up her
abode in you to receive her Son — which she can do
because of the sovereignty she has over all hearts — he
will be received by her in a perfect manner without
danger of being affronted or being forced to depart.
"God is in the midst of her. She shall not be moved." *

Tell her with confidence that all you have given
her of your possessions is little enough to honour her,
but that in Holy Communion you wish to give her the
same gift as the eternal Father gave her. Thus she will
feel more honoured than if you gave her all the wealth
in the world. Tell her, finally, that Jesus, whose love
for her is unique, still wishes to take his delight and
repose in her even in your soul, even though it is
poorer and less clean than the stable which he readily
entered because she was there. Beg her to lend you her
heart, saying, "O Mary, I take you for my all; give me
your heart."

* Ps. 45:6.

At Holy Communion

267. After the Our Father, when you are about to receive our Lord, say to him three times the prayer, "Lord, I am not worthy." Say it the first time as if you were telling the Eternal Father that because of your evil thoughts and your ingratitude to such a good Father, you are unworthy to receive his only-begotten Son, but that here is Mary, his handmaid, who acts for you and whose presence gives you a special confidence and hope in him.

268. Say to God the Son, "Lord, I am not worthy", meaning that you are not worthy to receive him because of your useless and evil words and your carelessness in his service, but nevertheless you ask him to have pity on you because you are going to usher him into the house of his Mother and yours, and you will not let him go until he has made it his home. Implore him to rise and come to the place of his repose and the ark of his sanctification. Tell him that you have no faith in your own merits, strength and preparedness, like Esau, but only in Mary, your Mother, just as Jacob had trust only in Rebecca his mother. Tell him that although you are a great sinner you still presume to approach him, supported by his holy Mother and adorned with her merits and virtues.

269. Say to the Holy Spirit, "Lord, I am not worthy." Tell him that you are not worthy to receive the masterpiece of his love because of your lukewarmness, wickedness, and resistance to his inspirations. But, nonetheless, you put all your confidence in Mary, his faithful Spouse, and you say with St. Bernard, "She is my greatest safeguard, the whole foundation of my hope." Beg him to overshadow Mary, his inseparable Spouse, once again. Her womb is as pure and her heart is as ardent as ever.

Tell him that if he does not enter your soul neither Jesus nor Mary will be formed there nor will it be a worthy dwelling for them.

After Holy Communion

270. After Holy Communion, close your eyes and recollect yourself. Then usher Jesus into the heart of Mary; you are giving him to his Mother who will receive him with great love and give him the place of honour, adore him profoundly, show him perfect love, embrace him intimately in spirit and in truth, and perform many offices for him of which we, in our ignorance, would know nothing.

271. Or, maintain a profoundly humble heart in the presence of Jesus dwelling in Mary. Or be in attendance like a slave at the gate of the royal palace, where the King is speaking with the Queen. While they are talking to each other, with no need of you, go in spirit to heaven and to the whole world, and call upon all creatures to thank, adore and love Jesus and Mary for you. "Come, let us adore."*

272. Or, ask Jesus living in Mary that his kingdom may come upon earth through his holy Mother. Ask for divine wisdom, divine love, the forgiveness of your sins, or any other grace, but always through Mary and in Mary. Cast a look of reproach upon yourself and say, "Lord, do not look at my sins, let your eyes see nothing in me but the virtues and merits of Mary." Remembering your sins, you may add, "I am my own worst enemy and I am guilty of all these sins," Or, "Deliver me from the unjust and deceitful man."† Or again, "Dear Jesus, you must increase in my soul and I must decrease."¹ "Mary, you must increase in me and

* Ps.94:6.   † Ps.42:1.   1 Cf.Jn.3:30.

I must always go on decreasing." "O Jesus and Mary, increase in me and increase in others around me."

273.   There   are   innumerable   other   thoughts   with which the Holy Spirit will inspire you, which he will make yours if you are thoroughly recollected and morti- fied, and constantly faithful to the great and sublime devotion which I have been teaching you. But remem- ber the more you let Mary act in your Communion the more Jesus will be glorified. The more you humble yourself and listen to Jesus and Mary in peace and silence — with no desire to see, taste or feel — then the more freedom you will give to Mary to act in Jesus' name and the more Jesus will act in Mary. For the just man lives everywhere by faith.* but especially in Holy Communion, which is an action of faith.

* Heb. 10:38; Rom. 1:17; Gal. 3:11.

ACT OF CONSECRATION

Eternal and Incarnate Wisdom, most lovable and adorable Jesus, true God and true man, only Son of the eternal Father and of Mary always virgin, I adore you profoundly, dwelling in the splendour of your Father from all eternity and in the virginal womb of Mary, your most worthy Mother, at the time of your Incarnation.

I thank you for having emptied yourself in assuming the condition of a slave to set me free from the cruel slavery of the evil one.

I praise and glorify you for having willingly chosen to obey Mary, your holy Mother, in all things, so that through her I may be your faithful slave of love.

But I must confess that I have not kept the vows and promises which I made to you so solemnly at my baptism. I have not fulfilled my obligations, and I do not deserve to be called your child or even your loving slave.

Since I cannot lay claim to anything except what merits your rejection and displeasure, I dare no longer approach the holiness of your majesty on my own. That is why I turn to the intercession and the mercy of your holy Mother, whom you yourself have given me to mediate with you. Through her I hope to obtain from you contrition and pardon for my sins, and that Wisdom whom I desire to dwell in me always.

I turn to you, then, Mary immaculate, living tabernacle of God. The eternal Wisdom, hidden in you, willed to receive the adoration of both men and angels.

I greet you as Queen of heaven and earth. All that is under God has been made subject to your sovereignty.

I call upon you as the unfailing refuge of sinners.

In your mercy you have never forsaken anyone.

Grant my desire for divine Wisdom and, in support of my petition, accept the promises and the offering of myself which I now make, conscious of my unworthiness.

I, an unfaithful sinner, renew and ratify today through you my baptismal promises. I renounce for ever Satan, his empty promises and his evil designs, and I give myself completely to Jesus Christ, the Incarnate Wisdom, to carry my cross after him for the rest of my life, and to be more faithful to him than I have been till now.

This day, with the whole court of heaven as witness, I choose you, Mary, as my Mother and Queen. I surrender and consecrate myself to you, body and soul, with all that I possess, both spiritual and material, even including the spiritual value of all my actions, past, present, and to come. I give you the full right to dispose of me and all that belongs to me, without any reservations, in whatever way you please, for the greater glory of God in time and throughout eternity.

Accept, gracious Virgin, this little offering of my slavery to honour and imitate that obedience which the eternal Wisdom willingly chose to have towards you, his Mother. I wish to acknowledge the authority which both of you have over this little worm and pitiful sinner. By it I wish also to thank God for the privileges bestowed on you by the Blessed Trinity. I solemnly declare that for the future I will try to honour and obey you in all things as your true slave of love.

O admirable Mother, present me to your dear Son as his slave now and for always, so that he who redeemed me through you, will now receive me through you.

Mother of mercy, grant me the favour of obtaining

the true Wisdom of God, and so make me one of those whom you love, teach and guide, whom you nourish and protect as your children and slaves.

Virgin most faithful, make me in everything so committed a disciple, imitator, and slave of Jesus, your Son, the Incarnate Wisdom, that I may become, through your intercession and example, fully mature with the fulness which Jesus possessed on earth, and with the fulness of his glory in heaven. Amen.

NOTES ON THE TEXT

2 'Hidden and unknown: According to St Jerome, that is the meaning of the Hebrew word *almah* (In Is. Proph. 3, 7).

4. 'Although he had given her the power': S.Th. III, q. 27, a.5, ad 3.

8. 'Holy, holy': *Sancta, sancta, sancta Maria, Dei Genitrix et Virgo.* St Bonav. (inter opuscula) Psalt. majus.

16. St. Augustine (inter subdititia), Serm. 215, in Redditione Symb.

18. 'Even at his death. . .': Cf. Benedict XV: 'Mary suffered and almost died with her suffering and dying Son. She abdicated her maternal rights for the salvation of men and, as much as she could, immolated her Son to appease the justice of God to such an extent that we can justifiably say that she redeemed the human race with her Son' *(Inter Sodalicia).*

II Vat. Council: 'Mary stood by the Cross suffering grievously with her only-begotten Son. There she united herself with a maternal heart to his sacrifice and lovingly consented to the immolation of this victim which she herself had brought forth and was also offering to the eternal Father *(Lumen Gentium, 58).* Cf. *Marialis Cultus,* 20.

24. 'Through her he applies his merits. . .': Richard of St Laurence, *De laudibus B.M.V.* L.2; Raymond Jordan (Idiota), *Piae lectiones de B.M.V.* in proem.

'His mystic channel': Richard of St Laurence, ibid.; St Bernard, In Nativ. B.M.V., Serm. de aquaeductu.

25. 'She distributes. . .: St Bernardine of Siena, Serm. de 12 Priv.; Serm. in Nativ. B.M.V.

Pius XII: 'She gives us her Son and with him she gives us all the help we need, for God wanted us to receive all through Mary (St Bernard)' *Mediator Dei,* 181).

32. 'Born of her': Cf. Pius X, 'We must consider ourselves as having our origin in Mary's womb, whence we were born as a body attached to the head *(Ad Diem illum,* 1903). Pius XII, 'She who was Mother of our Head according to the flesh became by a new title of sorrow and of glory the spiritual Mother of all his members' *(Mystici Corporis Christi,* 110). Paul VI, 'The faithful will be brought to a deeper realization of the brotherhood which unites all of them as sons and daughters of the Virgin Mary, who with a mother's love has cooperated in their rebirth and spiritual formation' *(Marialis Cultus,* 28).

33. St Augustine. De Virg. I, c.6; and De Symb. ad Catech., Serm. 4.

37. Cf. Pius XII, 'Her kingdom is as vast as that of her Son and of God, since nothing is excluded from her sovereignty' (Radio message to Fatima, 1946).

38. Cf. Pius XII, 'Jesus is the King of eternal ages by nature and by conquest. Through him, with him, and subordinate to him, Mary is queen by grace, by divine alliance, by special election (Radio message to Fatima, 1946).

'Queen of our Hearts'. Cf. a prayer indulgenced by the S. Penitentiary, 1924, 'Take and accept my whole being, O Mary, Queen of our hearts, and make me your slave with chains of love, that I may belong to you and may repeat in all truth, I belong entirely to Jesus through Mary'.

40. Cf. Pius XII, 'Devotion to the Virgin Mother of God, according to the opinion of the saints, is a sign of predestination' (Mediator Dei).

47. M. de Renty wrote a biography of Marie des Vallees, a celebrated mystic who died in 1656. St John Eudes was her spiritual director.

49. Denis the Areopagite. At the time of St Louis Marie, this apocryphal letter to St Paul was generally considered authentic.

66. 'Let no one presume...': *Non praesumat aliquis Deum se habere propitium qui benedictam matrem offensam habuerit* (William of Paris, 'De rhetorica divina').

67. The prayer of St Augustine, which the author gives in Latin, seems to have been composed of different extracts from the works of St Augustine or those attributed to him. The original compiler is unknown.

68. We belonged to the devil as slaves. Cf. S.Th.,III, q.48,a.4.

74. 'All that belongs to God...': *Quidquid Deo convenit per naturam, Mariae convenit per gratiam.* This principle of 'fittingness' was particularly brought out by Suarez, In III partem D. Thomae, q.27, a.2. Cf.Pius XII, '(The great Suarez) used to teach in Mariology that keeping in mind the standards of propriety, and where there is no repugnance on the part of Scripture, the mysteries of grace which God has wrought in the Virgin Mary must be measured not by ordinary laws but by the divine omnipotence' *(Munificentissimus Deus,* 1950).

'Just as Jesus and Mary have the same will...'. St John Damascene, (Hom.22 in Dorm. B.V.M.).

79. 'We have nothing in us but sin': Cf. 2 Council of Orange, *'Nemo habet de suo nisi mendacium et peccatum'* (Can. 22).

As regards the series of comparisons, 'prouder than peacocks', etc., which sometimes offend modern readers, St John Chrysostom gives a longer and more uncomplimentary list (Hom.4 in Math. n.8).

85. 'A mediator with the Mediator himself'; Cf. St Bernard, *'Opus enim est mediatore ad mediatorem Christum; nec alter nobis utilior quam Maria'* (Hom.5 in Assumpt.: Signum magnum, n.2). Serm. in Nativ. B.M.V., de aquaeductu, n.7.

89. Cf. St Leo the Great, *'Necesse est de mundano pulvere etiam religiosa corda sordescere'* (Serm.42, De Quadr. 4).

126. The promises of baptism are an act of *latria,* that is, due only to God, as is also their renewal. Therefore this consecration, which is a renewal of the baptismal promises, is an act of *latria.* This does not prevent us from offering them to God through our Lady.

127. St Thomas: *In baptismo vovent homines abrenuntiare diabolo et pompis ejus.* (S. Th. II-II, q.88,a.2). St Augustine: *Votum maximum nostrum quo vovimus nos in Christo esse mansuros* (Epis. 149 ad Paulinum, n.16). Canonist J. Calvinus: *Praecipuum votum est quod in baptismate facimus* (1553).

129. Catechism of the Council of Trent: *Parochus fidelem populum ad eam rationem cohortabitur ut sciat . . . aequum esse nos ipsos, non secus ac mancipia Redemptori nostro et Domino in perpetuum addicere et consecrare* (pars 1, c.3).

138. St Bernard: *Se toto totum me comparavit* (Serm. 22, de Diversis).

141. The four texts as given in Latin are:

Duo filii Mariae sunt, homo Deus et homo purus; unius corporaliter, et alterius spiritualiter mater est Maria (Conrad of Saxony, Speculum B.M.V.lect.3,parag. 1, a work which was attributed to St Bonaventure).

Haec est voluntas Dei, qui totum nos voluit habere per Mariam; ac proinde, si quid spei, si quid gratiae, si quid salutis ab ea noverimus redundare (St Bernard, Serm. in Nativ. B.M.V.: de aquaeductu, n.7 et 6).

Omnia dona, virtutes et gratiae ipsius Spiritus Sancti, quibus vult, quando vult, quomodo vult et quantum vult per ipsius manus administrantur (St Bernardine of Siena, Serm. de 12 Priv. 1.2,c.8).

Quia indignus eras cut daretur, datum est Mariae, ut per eam acciperes quidquid haberes (St Bernard, Serm 3 in Vigilia Nativ. Domini,n.10).

142. St Bernard: *Ut eodem alveo ad largitorem gratia redeat quo fluxit* (Serm. in Nativ. B.M.V.: de aquaeductu, n.18).

145. Abbot Rupert: *O Domina, Dei Genitrix, Maria, et incorrupta Mater Dei et hominis, non meis, sed tuis armatus meritis, cum ista Viro, scilicet Verbo Dei luctari, cupio* (Proem. in Cantica Cant. de Incarn. Domini).

St Augustine (inter opera), In fest. Assumpt. B.M.

149. St Bernard: *Modicum quod offerre desideras, manibus Mariae offerendum tradere cura, si non vis sustinere repulsam* (Serm. in Nativ. B.M.V.: de aquaeductu, n.18).

165. The saint mentioned is St Germanus of Constantinople, whose words were: *Nemo cogitatione Dei repletur nisi per te* (Serm.2 in Dormit. Deip.). He is also quoted in the following number.

167. 'As we are told by the Church': *Sola cunctas haereses interemisti in universo mundo* (formerly the Office of B.V.M., 3rd Nocturne).

174. St Bernard: *Ipse tenente, non corruis; ipsa protegente, non metuis; ipsa duce, non fatigaris; ipsa propitia, pervenis* (Hom.2 super Missus est, n.17).

St Bonaventure: *Virgo non solum in plenitudine sanctorum detinetur, sed etiam in plenitudine sanctos detinet, no plenitudo minuatur; detinet virtutes ne fugiant; detinet merita ne pereant; detinet gratias ne effluant; detinet daemones ne noceant; detinet Filium ne peccatores percutiat* (Inter opera S.Bonav., Conrad of Saxony, Speculum B.M.V. lect.7)

182. St John Damascene: *Spem tuam habens, o Dei-para, servabor; defensionem tuam possidens, non timebo; persequar inimicos meos et in fugam vertam, habens protectionem tuam et auxilium tuum; nam tibi devotum esse est arma quaedam salutis quae Deus his dat quos vult salvos fieri.* This text is not to be found in the Sermo de Annunt., which in any case is probably not authentic.

184. 'Full of mystery for us': It concerns the mystery of Jacob's predestination, for 'from his mother's womb he supplanted his brother' (Hos. 12:4). What happened later (the selling of the birth-right, the blessing of Isaac) only fulfils the plan of God.

186. 'They are very energetic. . .': *In terrenis fortes, in caelestibus debiles.* (St Gregory the Great, Moralium, L.32, c.22).

199. Abbot Guerric: *Ne credideris majoris esse felici-tatis habitare in sinu Abrahae quam in sinu Mariae, cum in eo Dominus posuerit thronum suum* (Serm. in Assumpt., n.4).

201. Cf. John XXIII: 'We are all protected by the sheltering and tender motherhood of the Virgin Mary, who performs for us the same services as every mother performs for her children. She loves us, she watches over us, she protects us, she intercedes for us' (Radio message, Lisieux, 1961).

206. The holy nun referred to was Mary of Agreda (1602-65), who published her revelations under the title 'The Mystical City of God'.

214. Now that our Lady is in heaven enjoying the beatific vision of God she does not possess the virtue of faith. St Louis merely means that as she has been com-missioned to distribute to men all graces and heavenly gifts, so likewise, with God's consent, she imparts to our faith the qualities her faith had on earth, that is, she makes it pure, lively, active, firm, and so on.

216.   St Bonaventure: *Ecce Domina salvatrix mea, fiducialiter agam, et non timebo, quia fortitudo mea, et laus mea in Domino es tu.* (Inter opera. Psalt. majus). *Tuus totus ego sum, et omnia mea tua sunt, o Virgo gloriosa, super omnia benedicta; ponam te ut signaculum super cor meum, quia fortis est ut mors dilectio tua* (Ibid.).

217.   St Ambrose: *Sit in singulis anima Mariae ut magnificet Dominum; sit in singulis spiritus Mariae ut exsultet in Deo* (Expos. in Luc.II, n.26).

The saintly man mentioned here seems to have been Fr Rigoleuc, a disciple of Fr Louis Lallemant.

221.   Cf. S.Th.: *Liquefactio importat quandam mollificationem qua exhibet se cor habile ut amatum in ipsum subintret* (I-II,q,38,a.5).

225.   Cf. Paul VI: 'In the Virgin Mary everything is relative to Christ and dependent upon him *(Marialis Cultus,* 25). Cf. *Lumen Gentium,* 67.

228.   St Bernard: *Cogita quid fueris, semen putridum; quid sis, vas stercorum; quid futurus sis, esca vermium* (St Bernard — inter opera — Meditationes piisimae de cognit. hum. condit., c.3, n.8).

255.   Jean le Charlier de Gerson (1363-1429) was chancellor of the University of Paris. The book referred to here is the *Tractatus XII super Magnificat.* Benzonio Rutilio was a bishop of Loreto, who died in 1613.

258.   St Alphonsus Rodriguez (1531-1617) was a Jesuit lay brother who was canonized in 1888. He is not to be confused with Father Alphonsus Rodriguez († 1616), the author of 'Christian Perfection'.

CONFRATERNITY OF MARY
QUEEN OF ALL HEARTS

ORIGIN: The Confraternity was first established in Canada, by Archbishop Duhamel of Ottawa, on March 25th. 1899. On April 28th. 1913 it was canonically erected as an Archconfraternity in Rome. Many centres have since been established in different countries.

OBJECT: The object of the confraternity is to establish within us the Reign of Mary as a means of establishing more perfectly the Reign of Jesus Christ in our souls.

CONDITIONS OF MEMBERSHIP:

1. To send in your name to be recorded in the official Register by the Father Director, who will send you a certificate of membership.

2. To prepare yourself to make the Act of Consecration to Jesus by the hands of Mary on a special day, preferably a feastday of Our Lady.

3. To perform a good work in honour of our Lady on the day of consecration.

4. To wear the badge of the Confraternity, which is a medal of our Lady, Queen of our hearts; but this is not required of those who wear a crucifix in some ostensible way.

PRACTICES:

To renew every morning the act of consecration to Jesus through Mary, at least by using the following formula: *'I belong wholly to you and all that I have I offer you, O most loving Jesus, through Mary, your holy Mother'*.

They should apply themselves to live always in dependance on Mary and to do all their actions in union with her.

INDULGENCES

On the occasion of the initial consecration (using the De Montfort formula) or, on the occasion of its renewal, a PLENARY INDULGENCE is granted, under the usual conditions (Confession, Communion and prayer for the intentions of the Holy Father). Also, a PLENARY INDULGENCE on the following days: 1 — The day of enrollment in the Confraternity; 2 — Holy Thursday; 3 — Christmas; 4 — Feast of the Annunciation; 5 — Feast of the Immaculate Conception (Dec. 8); 6 — St. Louis de Montfort's Feast day (April 28); 7 — Every First Saturday of the Month.

In answer to a petition by the Montfort Missionaries to the Sacred Penitentiary in Rome, the above indulgences were granted for a period of 10 years (as of Oct. 10, 1986), to the two Confraternities (Priests of Mary, Queen of All Hearts and the Confraternity of Mary, Queen of All Hearts), thus bringing them in line with the conditions laid down in the new ENCHIRIDION of Indulgences.

All members share in the merits and prayers and good works of both congregations founded by St. Louis Marie.

For further information one should write to:

Reverend Father Director,
The Confraternity,
26 So. Saxon Ave.
Bay Shore, N.Y. 11706

MONTFORTIAN CONGREGATIONS

Three congregations trace their foundation to Saint Louis de Montfort. The first, the *Daughters of Wisdom,* live out the loving search of Wisdom for wounded humanity through a variety of ministries, especially among those whom the world rejects and those alienated from the Church.

The missionary also yearned intensely for a company of vagabond preachers, enflamed by the Holy Spirit, totally trusting in Divine Providence, one with Mary in her loving surrender to God. Through this Company, Montfort firmly believed, the renewal of the Church would be brought about. This congregation of priests and brothers was given the name of the Company of the Holy Spirit and also the Company of Mary (which became its official name) for like Mary, the members of this Company are to be filled with the transforming power of the Holy Spirit. Today, this congregation is popularly known as the *Montfort Missionaries.*

At times the missionary would place some of the brothers of his small community in charge of teaching catechism to the poor; the group developed into the third community which recognizes Montfort as its founder, the teaching order of the *Brothers of Saint Gabriel.*

SUPPLEMENT

CONSECRATION

LITTLE CROWN

ROSARY

I

CONSECRATION TO JESUS THROUGH MARY

St. Louis De Montfort advises us to prepare for the consecration by exercises which certainly are not compulsory, but which assure its great efficacy because of the purity and other dispositions which they tend to develop in our souls.

Two different periods are assigned for these exercises: a preliminary period of twelve days during which we endeavor "to free ourselves from the spirit of the world"; and a second period of three weeks: the first devoted to the knowledge of ourselves, the second to that of the Blessed Virgin and the third to that of Jesus Christ.

These periods mentioned by St. Louis De Montfort do not constitute a rigorous and unchangeable division. According to circumstances, they may be lengthened or shortened. The faithful often take but three days to prepare for the annual renewal of their consecration.

The object of this consecration is to cast off the spirit of the world, which is contrary to that of Jesus Christ, in order to acquire fully the spirit of Jesus Christ through the Blessed Virgin. Hence the practices suggested by St. Louis De Montfort: renouncement of the world, knowledge of self, of the Blessed Virgin and of Jesus Christ.

FIRST PERIOD — TWELVE PRELIMINARY DAYS

Renouncement of the World

"The first part of the preparation should be employed in casting off the spirit of the world, which is contrary to that of Jesus Christ."

The spirit of the world consists essentially in the

denial of the supreme dominion of God, a denial which is manifested in practice by sin and disobedience; thus it is principally opposed to the spirit of Christ, which is also that of Mary.

It manifests itself by the concupiscence of the flesh, by the concupiscence of the eyes and by the pride of life; by disobedience to God's laws and the abuse of created things. Its works are, first, sin in all its forms; and then all else by which the devil leads to sin; works which bring error and darkness to the mind, and seduction and corruption to the will. Its pomps are the splendor and the charms employed by the devil to render sin alluring in persons, places and things.

Prayers to be said every day: Veni Creator and Ave Maris Stella.

Suitable reading for the twelve days: Gospel according to St. Matthew, chapters 5, 6, 7.

Imitation of Christ, Book I, chapters 13, 18, 25; Book III, chapters 10, 40.

Spiritual Exercises: Examine your conscience, pray, practice renouncement, mortification, purity of heart; this purity is the indispensable condition for contemplating God in heaven, to see Him on earth and to know Him by the light of faith.

Veni Creator

Come, O Creator Spirit blest!
And in our souls take up thy rest;
Come with Thy grace and heavenly aid,
To fill the hearts which Thou hast made.

Great Paraclete! To Thee we cry,
O highest gift of God most high!
O font of life! O fire of love!
And sweet anointing from above.

Thou in Thy sevenfold gifts art known,
The finger of God's hand we own;
The promise of the Father, Thou!
Who dost the tongue with power endow.

Kindle our senses from above,
And make our hearts o'erflow with love;
With patience firm and virtue high
The weakness of our flesh supply.

Far from us drive the foe we dread,
And grant us Thy true peace instead;
So shall we not, with Thee for guide,
Turn from the path of life aside.

O, may Thy grace on us bestow
The Father and the Son to know,
And Thee through endless times confessed
Of both the eternal Spirit blest.

All glory while the ages run
Be to the Father and the Son
Who rose from death; the same to Thee,
O Holy Ghost, eternally. Amen.

Magnificat

My soul doth magnify the Lord.
And my spirit hath rejoiced in God my Savior.
Because He hath regarded the humility of His handmaid; for behold, from henceforth all generations shall call me blessed.
Because He that is mighty hath done great things to me; and holy is His name.
And His mercy is from generation to generations to them that fear Him.

He hath showed might in His arm; He hath scattered the proud in the conceit of their heart.

He hath put down the mighty from their seat; and hath exalted the humble.

He hath filled the hungry with good things; and the rich he hath sent empty away.

He hath received Israel His servant, being mindful of His mercy.

As He spoke to our fathers, to Abraham and to his seed forever. Amen.

Glory be to the Father, etc.

Ave Maris Stella

Hail, bright star of ocean,
    God's own Mother blest,
Ever sinless Virgin,
    Gate of heavenly rest.

Taking that sweet Ave
    Which from Gabriel came,
Peace confirm within us,
    Changing Eva's name.

Break the captives' fetters,
    Light on blindness pour,
All our ills expelling,
    Every bliss implore.

Show thyself a Mother;
    May the Word Divine,
Born for us thy Infant,
    Hear our prayers through thine.

Virgin all excelling,
    Mildest of the mild,

Freed from guilt, preserve us,
   Pure and undefiled.
Keep our life all spotless,
   Make our way secure,
Till we find in Jesus
   Joy forevermore.

Through the highest heaven
   To the Almighty Three,
Father, Son and Spirit,
   One same glory be. Amen.

SECOND PERIOD — FIRST WEEK

Knowledge of Self

"During the first week they should employ all their prayers and pious actions in asking for a knowledge of themselves and for contrition of their sins; and they should do this in a spirit of humility."

During this week, we shall consider not so much the opposition that exists between the spirit of Jesus and ours, as the miserable and humiliating state to which our sins have reduced us. Moreover, the True Devotion being an easy, short, sure and perfect way to arrive at that union with Our Lord which is Christian perfection, we shall enter seriously upon this way, strongly convinced of our misery and helplessness. But how attain this without a knowledge of ourselves?

Prayers: Litany of the Holy Ghost. *Ave Maris Stella.* Litany of the Blessed Virgin.

Reading: Gospel according to St. Matthew, chapters 24, 25.

Gospel of St. Luke, chapters 11, 13, 16, 17, 18.

Imitation of Christ, Book I, chapter 24; Book II, chapter 5;

Book III, chapters 7, 8, 13, 20, 30, 47.

True Devotion nos. 78-82, 227, 228.

Spiritual Exercises: Prayers, examens, reflection, acts of renouncement of our own will, of contrition for our sins, of contempt of self — all performed at the feet of Mary, for it is from her we hope for light to know ourselves, and it is near her that we shall be able to measure the abyss of our miseries without despairing.

Litany of the Holy Ghost
(For private devotion only)

Lord, have mercy on us.

Christ, have mercy on us.

Lord, have mercy on us.

Father, all powerful, *have mercy on us.*

Jesus, Eternal Son of the Father, Redeemer of the world,
    save us.

Spirit of the Father and the Son, boundless life of both,
    sanctify us.

Holy Trinity, *hear us.*

Holy Ghost, Who proceedest from the Father and the Son,
    enter our hearts.

Holy Ghost, Who art equal to the Father and the Son, *enter
    our hearts.*

Promise of God the Father,

Ray of heavenly light,

Author of all good,

Source of heavenly water,

Consuming fire,

Ardent charity,

Spiritual unction,

Spirit of love and truth,

Spirit of wisdom and understanding,

Spirit of counsel and fortitude,

Have mercy on us.

Spirit of the fear of the Lord,
Spirit of grace and prayer,
Spirit of peace and meekness,
Spirit of modesty and innocence,
Holy Ghost, the Comforter,
Holy Ghost, the Sanctifier,
Holy Ghost, Who governest the Church,
Gift of God, the Most High,
Spirit Who fillest the universe,
Spirit of the adoption of the children of God,

Have mercy on us.

Holy Ghost, *inspire us with horror of sin.*
Holy Ghost, *come and renew the face of the earth.*
Holy Ghost, *shed Thy light in our souls.*
Holy Ghost, *engrave Thy law in our hearts.*
Holy Ghost, *inflame us with the flame of Thy love.*
Holy Ghost, *open to us the treasures of Thy graces.*
Holy Ghost, *teach us to pray well.*
Holy Ghost, *enlighten us with Thy heavenly inspirations.*
Holy Ghost, *lead us in the way of salvation.*
Holy Ghost, *grant us the only necessary knowledge.*
Holy Ghost, *inspire in us the practice of good.*
Holy Ghost, *grant us the merits of all virtues.*
Holy Ghost, *make us persevere in justice.*
Holy Ghost, *be Thou our everlasting reward.*
Lamb of God, Who takest away the sins of the world, *send us Thy Holy Ghost.*
Lamb of God, Who takest away the sins of the world, *pour down into our souls the gifts of the Holy Ghost.*
Lamb of God, Who takest away the sins of the world, *grant us the Spirit of wisdom and piety.*

V. *Come, Holy Ghost! Fill the hearts of Thy faithful.*
R. *And enkindle in them the fire of Thy love.*

Let us pray

Grant, O merciful Father, that Thy Divine Spirit enlighten, inflame and purify us, that He may penetrate us with His heavenly dew and make us fruitful in good works; through our Lord Jesus Christ, Thy Son, Who with Thee, in the unity of the same Spirit, liveth and reigneth forever and ever. Amen.

Litany of the Blessed Virgin

Lord, have mercy on us.
Christ, have mercy on us.
Lord, have mercy on us.
Christ, hear us.
Christ, graciously hear us.
God the Father of Heaven, *have mercy on us.*
God the Son, Redeemer of the world, *have mercy on us.*
God the Holy Ghost, *have mercy on us.*
Holy Trinity, one God, *have mercy on us.*
Holy Mary, *pray for us.*
Holy Mother of God,
Holy Virgin of virgins,
Mother of Christ,
Mother of divine grace,
Mother most pure,
Mother most chaste,
Mother inviolate,
Mother undefiled,
Mother most amiable,
Mother most admirable,
Mother of good counsel,
Mother of our Creator,
Mother of our Savior,
Virgin most prudent,
Virgin most venerable,
Virgin most renowned,
Virgin most powerful,
Virgin most merciful,
Virgin most faithful,
Mirror of justice,

Pray for us.

Seat of wisdom,
Cause of our joy,
Spiritual vessel,
Vessel of honor,
Singular vessel of devotion,
Mystical rose,
Tower of David,
Tower of ivory,
House of gold,
Ark of the covenant,
Gate of heaven,
Morning star,
Health of the sick,
Refuge of sinners,
Comforter of the afflicted,
Help of Christians,
Queen of angels,
Queen of patriarchs,
Queen of prophets,
Queen of Apostles,
Queen of martyrs,
Queen of confessors,
Queen of virgins,
Queen of all saints,
Queen conceived without original sin,
Queen assumed into heaven,
Queen of the most holy Rosary,
Queen of peace,

Pray for us.

Lamb of God, Who takest away the sins of the world, *spare us, O Lord.*

Lamb of God, Who takest away the sins of the world, *graciously hear us, O Lord.*

Lamb of God, Who takest away the sins of the world, *have mercy on us.*

V. Pray for us, O holy Mother of God.
R. That we may be made worthy of the promises of Christ.

Let us pray

Grant unto us, Thy servants, we beseech Thee, O Lord God, at all times to enjoy health of soul and body; and by the glorious intercession of Blessed Mary, ever virgin, when freed from the sorrows of this present life, to enter into that joy which hath no end. Through Christ our Lord. R. Amen.

SECOND WEEK

Knowledge of the Blessed Virgin

"They shall devote the second week to the knowledge of the Blessed Virgin."

We must unite ourselves to Jesus through Mary — this is the characteristic of our devotion; therefore Saint De Montfort asks that the second week be employed in acquiring a knowledge of the Blessed Virgin.

Mary is our sovereign and our mediatrix, our Mother and our Mistress. Let us then endeavor to know the effects of this royalty, of this mediation, and of this maternity, as well as the grandeurs and prerogatives which are the foundation or consequences thereof. Our Mother is also a perfect mold wherein we are to be molded in order to make her intentions and dispositions ours. This we cannot achieve without studying the interior life of Mary; namely, her virtues, her sentiments, her actions, her participation in the mysteries of Christ and her union with Him.

Prayers: Litany of the Holy Ghost. *Ave Maris Stella.* Litany of the Blessed Virgin. St. Louis De Montfort's Prayer to Mary. Recitation of the Rosary.

Reading: Gospel according to St. Luke, chapters 1, 2. Gospel according to St. John, chapter 2. *True Devotion,* nos. 1-48, 90-93, 105-182, 213-225. *Secret of Mary,* nos. 23-34.

Spiritual Exercises: Acts of love, pious affections for the Blessed Virgin, imitation of her virtues, especially her profound humility, her lively faith, her blind obedience, her continual mental prayer, her mortification in all things, her ardent charity, her heroic patience, her angelic sweetness and her divine wisdom; "these being," as St. Louis De Montfort says, "the ten principal virtues of the Blessed Virgin."

Litany of the Holy Ghost, page 162.
Ave Maris Stella, page 160.
Litany of the Blessed Virgin, page 164.

St. Louis De Montfort's Prayer to Mary

Hail Mary, beloved Daughter of the Eternal Father! Hail Mary, admirable Mother of the Son! Hail Mary, faithful Spouse of the Holy Ghost! Hail Mary, my dear Mother, my loving Mistress, my powerful sovereign! Hail my joy, my glory, my heart and my soul! Thou art all mine by mercy, and I am all thine by justice. But I am not yet sufficiently thine. I now give myself wholly to thee without keeping anything back for myself or others. If thou still seest in me anything which does not belong to thee, I beseech thee to take it and to make thyself the absolute Mistress of all that is mine. Destroy in me all that may be displeasing to God, root it up and bring it to nought; place and cultivate in me everything that is pleasing to thee.

May the light of thy faith dispel the darkness of my mind; may thy profound humility take the place of my pride; may thy sublime contemplation check the distractions of my wandering imagination; may thy continuous sight of God fill my memory with His presence; may the burning love of thy heart inflame the lukewarmness of mine; may thy virtues take the place of my sins; may thy merits be my only adornment in the sight of God and make up all that is wanting in me. Finally, dearly beloved Mother, grant, if it be possible, that I may have no other spirit but thine to know Jesus and His divine will; that I may have no other soul but thine to praise and glorify the Lord; that I may have no other heart but thine to love God with a love as pure and ardent as thine. I do not ask thee for visions, revelations, sensible devotion or spiritual pleasures. It is thy privilege to see God clearly; it is thy privilege to enjoy heavenly bliss; it is thy privilege to triumph gloriously in heaven at the right hand of thy Son and to hold absolute sway over angels, men and demons; it is thy privilege to dispose of all the gifts of God, just as thou willest.

Such is, O heavenly Mary, the "best part" which the Lord has given thee and which shall never be taken away from thee — and this thought fills my heart with joy. As for my part here below, I wish for no other than that which was thine: to believe sincerely without spiritual pleasures; to suffer joyfully without human consolation; to die continually to myself without respite; and to work zealously and unselfishly for thee until death as the humblest of thy servants. The only grace I beg thee to obtain for me is that every day and every moment of my life I may say: Amen — Amen — so be it, to all that thou art now doing in heaven; Amen — so be it, to all that thou art doing in my soul, so that thou alone mayest fully glorify Jesus in me for time and eternity. Amen.

THIRD WEEK

Knowledge of Jesus Christ

"During the third week, they shall apply themselves to the study of Jesus Christ."

What is to be studied in Christ? First the Man-God, His grace and glory; then His rights to sovereign dominion over us; since, after having renounced Satan and the world, we have taken Jesus Christ for our "Lord." What next shall be the object of our study? His exterior actions and also His interior life; namely, the virtues and acts of

His Sacred Heart; His association with Mary in the mysteries of the Annunciation and Incarnation, during His infancy and hidden life, at the feast of Cana and on Calvary.

Prayers: Litany of the Holy Ghost. *Ave Maris Stella.* Litany of the Holy Name of Jesus or of the Sacred Heart. St. Louis De Montfort's Prayer to Jesus. The prayer: *O Jesus living in Mary.*

Reading: Gospel according to St. Matthew, chapters 26, 27. Gospel according to St. John, chapters 13 et ff.

Imitation of Christ, Book II, chapters 7, 11, 12; Book III, chapters 5, 6, 56; Book IV, chapters 1, 8, 13.

True Devotion, nos. 60-67, 183, 212, 226-265.

Spiritual Exercises: Acts of love of God, thanksgiving for the blessings of Jesus, contrition and resolution.

Litany of the Holy Ghost, page 162.

Ave Maris Stella, page 160.

Litany of the Holy Name of Jesus

Lord, have mercy on us.
Christ, have mercy on us.
Lord, have mercy on us.
Jesus hear us.
Jesus, graciously hear us.
God the Father of heaven,
God the Son, Redeemer of the world,
God the Holy Ghost,
Holy Trinity, one God,
Jesus, Son of the living God,
Jesus, splendor of the Father,
Jesus, brightness of eternal light,
Jesus, King of glory,
Jesus, son of justice,
Jesus, Son of the Virgin Mary,
Jesus, most amiable,
Jesus, most admirable,

Have mercy on us.

Jesus, mighty God,
Jesus, Father of the world to come,
Jesus, angel of the great council,
Jesus, most powerful,
Jesus, most patient,
Jesus, most obedient,
Jesus, meek and humble of heart,
Jesus, lover of chastity,
Jesus, lover of us,
Jesus, God of peace,
Jesus, author of life,
Jesus, model of virtues,
Jesus, lover of souls,
Jesus, our God,
Jesus, our refuge,
Jesus, Father of the poor,
Jesus, treasure of the faithful,
Jesus, Good Shepherd,
Jesus, true light,
Jesus, eternal wisdom,
Jesus, infinite goodness,
Jesus, our way and our life,
Jesus, joy of angels,
Jesus, King of patriarchs,
Jesus, master of Apostles,
Jesus, teacher of Evangelists,
Jesus, strength of martyrs,
Jesus, light of confessors,
Jesus, purity of virgins,
Jesus, crown of all saints,

Have mercy on us.

Be merciful, *spare us, O Jesus.*
Be merciful, *graciously hear us, O Jesus*
From all evil,
From all sin,
From Thy wrath,
From the snares of the devil,
From the spirit of fornication,

Jesus, deliver us.

From everlasting death,
From the neglect of Thine inspirations,
Through the mystery of Thy holy Incarnation,
Through Thy nativity,
Through Thine infancy,
Through Thy most divine life,
Through Thy labors,
Through Thine agony and Passion,
Through Thy cross and dereliction,
Through Thy sufferings,
Through Thy death and burial,
Through Thy Resurrection,
Through Thine Ascension,
Through Thine institution of the most Holy Eucharist,
Through Thy joys,
Through Thy glory,

Jesus, deliver us.

Lamb of God, Who takest away the sins of the world, *spare us, O Jesus.*

Lamb of God, Who takest away the sins of the world, *graciously hear us, O Jesus.*

Lamb of God, Who takest away the sins of the world, *have mercy on us.*

Jesus, hear us,
Jesus, graciously hear us.

Let us pray

O Lord Jesus Christ, Who hast said: Ask and ye shall receive; seek and ye shall find; knock and it shall be opened unto you; grant, we beseech Thee, to us who ask the gift of Thy divine love, that we may ever love Thee with all our hearts, and in all our words and actions, and never cease praising Thee.

Give us, O Lord, a perpetual fear and love of Thy holy Name; for Thou never failest to govern those whom Thou dost solidly establish in Thy love. Who livest and reignest world without end. Amen.

Litany of the Sacred Heart

Lord, have mercy on us.
Christ, have mercy on us.
Lord, have mercy on us.
Christ, hear us.
Christ, graciously hear us.
God the Father of Heaven,
God the Son, Redeemer of the world,
God the Holy Ghost,
Holy Trinity, one God,
Heart of Jesus, Son of the Eternal Father,
Heart of Jesus, formed by the Holy Ghost in the womb of
      the Virgin Mother,
Heart of Jesus, substantially united with the Word of God,
Heart of Jesus, of infinite majesty,
Heart of Jesus, holy temple of God,
Heart of Jesus, tabernacle of the Most High,
Heart of Jesus, house of God and gate of heaven,
Heart of Jesus, burning furnace of charity,
Heart of Jesus, abode of justice and love,
Heart of Jesus, full of goodness and love,
Heart of Jesus, abyss of all virtues,
Heart of Jesus, most worthy of all praise,
Heart of Jesus, King and center of all hearts,
Heart of Jesus, in whom are all the treasures of wisdom
      and knowledge,
Heart of Jesus, in whom dwells all the fulness of divinity,
Heart of Jesus, in whom the Father was well pleased,
Heart of Jesus, whose fulness we have all received,
Heart of Jesus, desire of the everlasting hills,
Heart of Jesus, patient and most merciful,
Heart of Jesus, enriching all who invoke Thee,
Heart of Jesus, fountain of life and holiness,
Heart of Jesus, propitiation for our sins,
Heart of Jesus, loaded down with opprobrium,
Heart of Jesus, bruised for our offenses,

Have mercy on us.

Heart of Jesus, obedient unto death,
Heart of Jesus, pierced with a lance,
Heart of Jesus, source of all consolation,
Heart of Jesus, our life and resurrection,
Heart of Jesus, our peace and reconciliation,
Heart of Jesus, victim for sin,
Heart of Jesus, salvation of those who trust in Thee,
Heart of Jesus, hope of those who die in Thee,
Heart of Jesus, delight of all the saints,

Have mercy on us.

Lamb of God, Who takest away the sins of the world, *spare us, O Lord.*

Lamb of God, Who takest away the sins of the world, *graciously hear us, O Lord.*

Lamb of God, Who takest away the sins of the world, *have mercy on us.*

V. *Jesus, meek and humble of heart.*
R. *Make our hearts like unto Thine.*

Let us pray

Almighty and everlasting God, graciously regard the Heart of Thy well-beloved Son and the acts of praise and satisfaction which He renders Thee on behalf of us sinners, and through their merit grant pardon to us who implore Thy mercy, in the name of Thy Son Jesus Christ; Who liveth and reigneth with Thee in the unity of the Holy Spirit, world without end.
R. Amen.

St. Louis De Montfort's Prayer to Jesus

O most loving Jesus, deign to let me pour forth my gratitude before Thee, for the grace Thou hast bestowed upon me in giving me to Thy holy Mother through the devotion of Holy Bondage, that she may be my advocate in the presence of Thy majesty and my support in my extreme misery. Alas, O Lord! I am so wretched that without this dear Mother I should be certainly lost. Yes, Mary is necessary for me at Thy side and everywhere: that she may appease thy just wrath, because I have so often offended Thee; that she may save me from the eternal punishment of Thy justice, which I deserve; that she may contemplate Thee, speak to Thee, pray to Thee, approach Thee and please Thee; that she may help me to save my soul and the souls of others; in short, Mary is necessary for me that I may always do Thy holy will and seek Thy greater glory in all things. Ah, would that I could proclaim throughout the whole world the mercy that Thou hast shown to me! Would that everyone might know I should be already damned, were it not for Mary! Would that I might offer worthy thanksgiving for so great a blessing! Mary is in me. Oh, what a treasure! Oh, what a consolation! And shall I not be entirely hers? Oh, what ingratitude! My dear Savior, send me death rather than such a calamity, for I would rather die than live without belonging entirely to Mary. With St. John the Evangelist at the foot of the cross, I have taken her a thousand times for my own and as many times have given myself to her; but if I have not yet done it as Thou, dear Jesus, dost wish, I now renew this offering as Thou dost desire me to renew it. And if Thou seest in my soul or my body anything that does not belong to this august princess, I pray Thee to take it and cast it far from me, for whatever in me does not belong to Mary is unworthy of Thee.

O Holy Spirit, grant me all these graces. Plant in my soul the Tree of true Life, which is Mary; cultivate it and tend it so that it may grow and blossom and bring forth the fruit of life in abundance. O Holy Spirit, give me great devotion to Mary, Thy faithful spouse; give me great confidence in her maternal heart and an abiding refuge in her mercy, so that by her Thou mayest truly form in me Jesus Christ, great and mighty, unto the fullness of His perfect age. Amen.

O Jesus Living in Mary

O Jesus living in Mary,
come and live in Thy servants,
In the spirit of Thy holiness,
In the fulness of Thy might,
In the truth of Thy virtues,
In the perfection of Thy ways,
In the communion of Thy mysteries,
Subdue every hostile power
In Thy spirit, for the glory of the Father. Amen.

The Consecration

"At the end of the three weeks," says St. Louis De Montfort, "they shall go to confession and to Communion, with the intention of giving themselves to Jesus Christ in the quality of slaves of love, by the hands of Mary. After Communion, which they should try to make according to the method given further on, they should recite the formula of their consecration, which they will also find further on. They ought to write it, or have it written, unless they have a printed copy of it; and they should sign it the same day they have made it. It would be well also that on that day they should pay some tribute to Jesus Christ and our Blessed Lady, either as a penance for their past unfaithfulness to the vows of their Baptism or as a testimony of their dependence on the dominion of Jesus and Mary. This tribute ought to be according to the devotion and ability of everyone; such as, a fast, a mortification, an alms or a candle. If they had but a pin to give in homage, yet gave it with good heart, it would be enough for Jesus, Who looks only at one's good will. Once a year at least, on the same day, they should renew the same consecration, observing the same practices during the three weeks. They might also once a month, or even once a day, renew all they have done in these few words: "I am all Thine and all that I have belongs to Thee, O my sweet Jesus, through Mary, Thy holy Mother.' "

For formula of Consecration, see p. 141.

II

THE LITTLE CROWN OF THE BLESSED VIRGIN

St. John the Evangelist saw a woman crowned with twelve stars, clothed with the sun, and the moon under her feet. According to the commentators, this woman is the Blessed Virgin Mary, with her virtues and her privileges, especially that of her divine maternity. Thus originated the *Little Crown of the Twelve Stars of the Blessed Virgin Mary,* which St. Joseph Calasanctius, St. John Berchmans and many other saints made it a practice to recite frequently.

In order to make this prayer more attractive, St. Louis De Montfort added to each *Hail Mary* one of the praises of the Blessed Virgin, with the invocation "Rejoice, O Virgin Mary; rejoice a thousand times."

It is this prayer which St. Louis De Montfort gave to his religious families (the Montfort Fathers and the Daughters of Wisdom) as their morning prayer. He also recommends it to all those who embrace the devotion of the holy and loving slavery of Jesus through Mary.

LITTLE CROWN OF THE BLESSED VIRGIN MARY
I. Crown of Excellence

(To honor the divine maternity of the Blessed Virgin, her ineffable virginity, her purity without stain and her innumerable virtues.)

1. *Our Father.*
   Hail Mary.
   Blessed art thou, O Virgin Mary, who didst bear the

Lord, the Creator of the world; thou didst give birth to Him Who made thee and remainest a Virgin forever.
Rejoice, O Virgin Mary.
Rejoice a thousand times!

2. *Hail Mary.*
O holy and immaculate Virgin, I know not with what praise to extoll thee, since thou didst bear in thy womb the very One Whom the heavens cannot contain.
Rejoice, O Virgin Mary,
Rejoice a thousand times!

3. *Hail Mary.*
Thou art all fair, O Virgin Mary, and there is no stain in thee.
Rejoice, O Virgin Mary,
Rejoice a thousand times!

4. *Hail Mary.*
Thy virtues, O Virgin, surpass the stars in number.
Rejoice, O Virgin Mary,
Rejoice a thousand times!
Glory be to the Father.

II. Crown of Power.

(To honor the royalty of the Blessed Virgin, her magnificence, her universal mediation and the strength of her rule.)

5. *Our Father.*
Hail Mary.
Glory be to thee, O empress of the world! Bring us with thee to the joys of heaven.
Rejoice, O Virgin Mary,
Rejoice a thousand times!

6. *Hail Mary.*
   Glory be to thee, O treasure-house of the Lord's graces!
   Grant us a share in thy riches.
   Rejoice, O Virgin Mary,
   Rejoice a thousand times!

7. *Hail Mary.*
   Glory be to thee, O Mediatrix between God and man!
   Through thee may the Almighty be favorable to us.
   Rejoice, O Virgin Mary,
   Rejoice a thousand times!

8. *Hail Mary.*
   Glory be to thee who destroyest heresies and crushest
   demons! Be thou our loving guide.
   Rejoice, O Virgin Mary,
   Rejoice a thousand times!
   Glory be to the Father.

III. Crown of Goodness

(To honor the mercy of the Blessed Virgin toward
sinners, the poor, the just and the dying.)

9. *Our Father.*
   Hail Mary.
   Glory be to thee, O refuge of sinners! Intercede for us
   with God.
   Rejoice, O Virgin Mary,
   Rejoice a thousand times!

10. *Hail Mary.*
    Glory be to thee, O Mother of orphans! Render the Al-
    might favorable to us.
    Rejoice, O Virgin Mary,
    Rejoice a thousand times!

11. *Hail Mary.*
Glory be to thee, O joy of the just! Lead us with thee to the joys of heaven.
Rejoice, O Virgin Mary,
Rejoice a thousand times!

12. *Hail Mary.*
Glory be to thee who art ever ready to assist us in life and in death! Lead us with thee to the kingdom of heaven!
Rejoice, O Virgin Mary,
Rejoice a thousand times!
Glory be to the Father.

Let us pray

Hail, Mary, Daughter of God the Father; Hail, Mary, Mother of God the Son; Hail, Mary, Spouse of the Holy Ghost; Hail, Mary, Temple of the most Holy Trinity; Hail, Mary, my Mistress, my treasure, my joy, Queen of my heart; my Mother, my life, my sweetness, my dearest hope, yea, my heart and my soul! I am all thine and all that I have is thine, O Virgin blessed above all things! Let thy soul be in me to magnify the Lord; let thy spirit be in me to rejoice in God. Set thyself, O faithful Virgin, as a seal upon my heart, that in thee and through thee I may be found faithful to God. Receive me, O gracious Virgin, among those whom thou lovest and teachest, whom thou leadest, nourishest and protectest as thy children. Grant that for love of thee I may despise all earthly consolations and ever cling to those of heaven; until through the Holy Ghost, thy faithful Spouse, and through thee, His faithful Spouse, Jesus Christ thy Son be formed in me for the glory of the Father. Amen.

III

THE HOLY ROSARY

THE METHOD OF ST. LOUIS DE MONTFORT

I unite with all the saints in heaven, with all the just on earth and with all the faithful here present. I unite with Thee, O my Jesus, in order to praise worthily Thy holy Mother and to praise Thee in her and through her. I renounce all the distractions I may have during this Rosary which I wish to say with modesty, attention and devotion, just as if it were to be the last of my life.

We offer Thee, O most Holy Trinity, this *Creed* in honor of all the mysteries of our Faith; this *Our Father* and these three *Hail Marys* in honor of the unity of Thy Essence and the Trinity of Thy Persons. We ask of Thee a lively faith, a firm hope and an ardent charity. Amen.

I believe in God, etc.

THE FIVE JOYFUL MYSTERIES

1. The Annunciation

We offer Thee, O Lord Jesus, this first decade in honor of Thy Incarnation in Mary's womb, and we ask of Thee, through this Mystery and through her intercession, a profound humility. Amen.

Our Father, etc.

May the grace of the Mystery of the Annunciation como down into our souls. Amen.

2. The Visitation

We offer Thee, O Lord Jesus, this second decade in honor of the Visitation of Thy holy Mother to her cousin St. Elizabeth and the sanctification of St. John the Baptist, and we ask of Thee, through this Mystery and through the intercession of Thy holy Mother, charity towards our neighbor. Amen.

Our Father, etc.

May the grace of the Mystery of the Visitation come down into our souls. Amen.

3. The Nativity

We offer Thee, O Lord Jesus, this third decade in honor of Thy Nativity in the stable of Bethlehem, and we ask of Thee, through this Mystery and through the intercession of Thy holy Mother, detachment from the things of the world, contempt of riches and love of poverty. Amen.

Our Father, etc.

May the grace of the Mystery of the Nativity come down into our souls. Amen.

4. The Presentation in the Temple

We offer Thee, O Lord Jesus, this fourth decade in honor of Thy Presentation in the Temple and the Purification of Mary, and we ask of Thee, through this Mystery and through the intercession of Thy holy Mother, purity of body and soul. Amen.

Our Father, etc.

May the grace of the Mystery of the Presentation in the Temple come down into our souls. Amen.

5. The Finding of Our Lord in the Temple

We offer Thee, O Lord Jesus, this fifth decade in honor of Mary's finding Thee in the Temple, and we ask of Thee, through this Mystery and through her intercession, the gift of true wisdom. Amen.

Our Father, etc.

May the grace of the Mystery of the Finding of Our Lord in the Temple come down into our souls. Amen.

THE FIVE SORROWFUL MYSTERIES

1. The Agony in the Garden

We offer Thee, O Lord Jesus, this sixth decade in honor of Thy Agony in the Garden of Olives, and we ask of Thee, through this Mystery and through the intercession of Thy holy Mother, contrition for our sins. Amen.

Our Father, etc.

May the grace of the Mystery of the Agony in the Garden come down into our souls. Amen.

2. The Scourging

We offer Thee, O Lord Jesus, this seventh decade in honor of Thy bloody Scourging, and we ask of Thee, through this Mystery and through the intercession of Thy holy Mother, the grace of mortifying our senses. Amen.

Our Father, etc.

May the grace of the Mystery of the Scourging come down into our souls. Amen.

3. The Crowning with Thorns

We offer Thee, O Lord Jesus, this eighth decade in honor of Thy being crowned with thorns and we ask of Thee, through this Mystery and through the intercession of Thy holy Mother, contempt of the world. Amen.

Our Father, etc.

May the grace of the Mystery of the Crowning with Thorns come down into our souls. Amen.

4. The Carrying of the Cross

We offer Thee, O Lord Jesus, this ninth decade in honor of Thy carrying of the cross, and we ask of Thee, through this Mystery and through the intercession of Thy holy Mother, patience in bearing our crosses. Amen.

Our Father, etc.

May the grace of the Mystery of the Carrying of the Cross come down into our souls. Amen.

5. The Crucifixion

We offer Thee, O Lord Jesus, this tenth decade in honor of Thy Crucifixion and ignominious death on Calvary; we ask of Thee, through this Mystery and through the intercession of Thy holy Mother, the conversion of sinners, the perseverance of the just and the relief of the souls in purgatory. Amen.

Our Father, etc.

May the grace of the Mystery of the Crucifixion come down into our souls. Amen.

THE FIVE GLORIOUS MYSTERIES

1. The Resurrection

We offer Thee, O Lord Jesus, this eleventh decade in honor of Thy glorious Resurrection, and we ask of Thee, through this Mystery and through the intercession of Thy holy Mother, love of God and fervor in Thy service. Amen.

Our Father, etc.

May the grace of the Mystery of the Resurrection come down into our souls. Amen.

2. The Ascension

We offer Thee, O Lord Jesus, this twelfth decade in honor of Thy triumphant Ascension and we ask of Thee, through this Mystery and through the intercession of Thy holy Mother, an ardent desire for heaven, our true home. Amen.

Our Father, etc.

May the grace of the Mystery of the Ascension come down into our souls. Amen.

3. The Descent of the Holy Ghost

We offer Thee, O Lord Jesus, this thirteenth decade in honor of the Mystery of Pentecost, and we ask of Thee, through this Mystery and through the intercession of Thy holy Mother, the coming of the Holy Ghost into our souls. Amen.

Our Father, etc.

May the grace of the Mystery of Pentecost come down into our souls. Amen.

4. The Assumption

We offer Thee, O Lord Jesus, this fourteenth decade in honor of the resurrection and triumphant Assumption of Thy holy Mother into heaven and we ask of Thee, through this Mystery and through her intercession, a tender devotion for so good a Mother. Amen.

Our Father, etc.

May the grace of the Mystery of the Assumption come down into our souls. Amen.

5. The Coronation of the Blessed Virgin

We offer Thee, O Lord Jesus, this fifteenth decade in honor of the Coronation of Thy holy Mother, and we ask of Thee, through this Mystery and through her intercession, perseverance in grace and a crown of glory hereafter. Amen.

Our Father, etc.

May the grace of the Mystery of the Coronation of the Blessed Virgin come down into our souls. Amen.

Hail Mary, beloved Daughter of the Eternal Father, admirable Mother of the Son, faithful Spouse of the Holy Ghost, august Temple of the most Holy Trinity! Hail, sovereign princess, to whom all owe subjection in heaven and on earth! Hail, sure refuge of sinners, our Lady of mercy, who hast never refused any request. All sinful though I am, I cast myself at thy feet and beseech thee to obtain from Jesus, thy beloved Son, contrition and pardon for all my sins, as well as the gift of divine wisdom. I consecrate myself entirely to thee with all that I have. I choose thee today for my Mother and Mistress. Treat me, then, as the least of thy children and the most obedient of thy servants. Listen, my princess, listen to the sighs of a heart that desires to love and serve thee faithfully. Let it never be said that of all those who have had recourse to thee, I was the first to be abandoned. O my hope, O my life, O my faithful and Immaculate Virgin Mary, defend me, nourish me, hear me, teach me and save me. Amen.